DATE DUE

	MAY 03 2010
NEW BOOK	DEC 13 2012
Sent 11-7-94	JUN 06 2013
JAN 09 1995	
FEB 21 995	
MAY 30 1995	
Sent 6-28-95	
NOV 07 1995	
JAN 29 1996	
FEB 07 1996	
sent 4-11-96	
Sent 9/10/96	
MAY 12 1997	
AUG 25 1997	
MAY 01 2000	
JUN 05 2000	
FEB 25 2002	

The Electric
Geisha

The Electric Geisha

EXPLORING JAPAN'S POPULAR CULTURE

Edited by
Atsushi Ueda

Translated by
Miriam Eguchi

KODANSHA INTERNATIONAL
Tokyo • New York • London

NOTE: *The names of historical figures are given in the traditional manner, surname preceding given name. All other names follow the Western order.*

Photo credits: The authors and publisher are grateful to the following people and institutions for permission to reproduce the illustrated material found in these pages: page 19, Dana Levy; page 22, Maspro Denkoh Art Gallery; page 32, Shūji Hidaka; pages 40 and 62, Hans Sautter, photographer; page 49, Ikenobō; page 61, Tokyo National Museum; pages 94 and 209 (both), Kiyohide Shibashita, photographer; page 143, National Archives, "Hyakushō Seisui-ki"; page 148, the Japanese Mint Bureau, "Kinza-ezu"; page 194, Okinawa Prefectural Museum, "Konrei-shuen-no-zu"; page 216, Machida City Museum of Graphic Arts, "Imayō-mitate-Shinōkōshō"; page 232, June magazine, K.K. Sun, publisher; page 236 (above), Hakusensha, Imari Sumiko Collection, *vol. 2, "Itoshiki Akaki Daichi."*

Distributed in the United States by Kodansha America, Inc., 114 Fifth Avenue, New York, New York 10011, and in the United Kingdom and continental Europe by Kodansha Europe Ltd., 95 Aldwych, London WC2B 4JF.

Published by Kodansha International Ltd., 17–14 Otowa 1-chome, Bunkyo-ku, Tokyo 112, and Kodansha America, Inc.

Library of Congress Cataloging-in-Publication Data
Ueda, Atsushi, 1930–
The electric geisha: exploring Japanese popular culture
/ Atsushi Ueda, ed.; translated
by Miriam Eguchi.
1. Japan—Civilization—1945– I. Title.
DS822.5.U2913 1994 952.04–dc20 93-37752 CIP

ISBN 4-7700-1753-7

CONTENTS

Preface

The publication of *The Electric Geisha* brings to a close five years of work by participating essayists. In 1988 we formed a research group in order to explore the links between popular culture and the Japanese city, which exhibits many qualities not found in other cities in Asia or the rest of the world. Each of us traced his or her subject from that pivotal epoch in Japanese history called the Edo period (1600–1867), an age of relative peace, to the present. At times, we reached back even farther.

All this was done under an umbrella concept we called the "mass city," a term coined to designate a type of modern and pre-modern city found throughout the world. (The final essay of this book examines this theme in detail.) In Japan's case, the emergence of the mass city spawned or greatly influenced various facets of the popular culture.

I hope the present volume captures the essence of our efforts to illuminate some intriguing aspects of Japanese culture. We have attempted to bring a new perspective to many of the subjects discussed. At the very least, I believe we have opened up fresh avenues of thought.

As with most books of such wide scope, a number of people generously contributed their time and energy. I would like to express my gratitude to the following: To Nobuaki Mochizuki and Nihon Seimei Zaidan for their support; to all the contributing essayists; to Michitarō Tada and Yoshisuke Nakaoka; to Miriam Eguchi, our thorough and patient translator; to Peter Dowling, Adrian Waller, and Elizabeth Wood; and finally to Shigeyoshi Suzuki, Yūichiro Kaihotsu, and Barry Lancet at Kodansha International.

Atsushi Ueda
Kyoto, Japan

Introduction

Several years ago when I first translated some of Professor Atsushi Ueda's work, I discovered that he was not only a well-known architect, but a social commentator with some very original views. Even so, the present collection took me by surprise. I had expected twenty or so academic studies of unrelated social phenomena, but what unfolds in these pages is a kaleidoscopic vista of life in Japan's pulsating cities over the past four hundred years.

Each piece delves deeply into a specific aspect of modern Japanese culture, with emphasis on the historical. We are taken back in time to the world of seventeenth- and eighteenth-century Japanese cities, thriving centers of activity with populations exceeding most major cities in the West. It was a time of samurai and geisha, kimono and palanquins, pleasure quarters and Kabuki theater. The townspeople we meet here are brimming with vitality—they live for the moment, crave every manner of diversion, and would rather spend the little money they earn on pleasure and aesthetically pleasing possessions than save toward an uncertain future. We see rows of makeshift wooden dwellings and shops in crowded, mazelike neighborhoods clustering around castle-town walls. Everywhere there is bustling commercial activity. With brisk staccato shouts, street vendors peddle everything from quick meals to woodblock news-sheets, and shopkeepers tempt passersby with colorful displays. People of all ages congregate to socialize in bathhouses, teashops, or at firefighting "events."

From the vitality of these times emerged a dynamic popular culture that continues to thrive in modern Japan. At first glance the essays in *The Electric Geisha* seem to cover a wide range of diverse topics, yet running through them like strands of a tapestry—appearing, reappearing, and connecting each essay to the others—are the social and psychological themes that make history come alive.

Why did Japanese popular culture flourish in the Edo period? How did it begin?

Japanese recorded history goes back only as far as the sixth century, when Chinese culture, including written characters and Buddhism, were imported from the continent. During the Heian period (794–1185), the court nobles were the main stimulus behind the development of an elite Japanese culture that included literature, music, dance, elaborate dress, and esoteric Buddhism. Meanwhile, although the imperial line continued unbroken, the actual ruling power shifted from emperors and empresses to aristocratic regents, retired emperors, and finally to military leaders in the late twelfth century.

After the military took power, the country suffered four centuries of strife and disunity, climaxing in the Warring States period of 1442–1558. The various warlords throughout the country were supported in their military campaigns by their samurai retainers, the peasants in their domains, and powerful Buddhist sects with whom they formed alliances. During the sixteenth century, the nation was finally unified under central control through the brilliant and often ruthless tactics of three successive leaders: Oda Nobunaga (1534–82), Toyotomi Hideyoshi (1536–98), and Tokugawa Ieyasu (1542–1616). All three were ambitious warlords who rose to a position of national power by overthrowing the lords they were supposed to be serving, one after another, beginning at the local level. As each of the three came to power, he was determined not to meet the same fate as the superiors over whom he himself had triumphed. Thus Nobunaga systematically destroyed the power of the Buddhist sects, and Hideyoshi separated the samurai from the peasants by moving the former to castle towns. The process was completed by Ieyasu, who took power as the first Tokugawa shogun in 1603, and defeated the Toyotomi family, his last rivals, in 1615. This was the beginning of the Edo, or Tokugawa, period.

As a result of these men's policies, hundreds of castle towns were created all over Japan. The samurai, who lived within the castle walls, manned the national and regional bureaucracies. Outside the walls lived merchants, artisans, laborers, and assorted transients, who together composed what Professor Ueda's research group calls "the masses."

The administrative policies enforced by Ieyasu and his successors were designed to make insurrections impossible by preventing horizontal alliances of any kind, and keeping the various sectors of the population segregated from each other. People were required to spy on each other, reporting anything out of the ordinary to the authorities. It was obligatory for all lords of domains to spend alternate years or half-years at the shogunate headquarters in Edo with their retinues. Thus no individual or group could build up an economic or military base at home strong enough to pose a threat to the central government.

The populace was divided into four classes: samurai, farmers, artisans, and merchants. They were differentiated from each other by strict regulations of dress, location and type of residence, forms of transportation, and many other aspects of daily life. Not included in these four classes were the nobility, and the outcasts who did jobs considered defiling, such as those connected with death, animal slaughter, or sanitation.

Although the people had to endure a regime of totalitarian control that imposed severe restrictions on their lifestyle and social mobility, they did have relative peace and stability for two-and-a-half centuries. The majority of the population were far from affluent, but neither were they starving or homeless. Without wars to worry about, and with bare survival no longer an issue, it is not surprising that they had a great deal of surplus energy to devote to the creation of their own culture.

The word "culture" here is used in the broadest sense—material culture, economics, politics, arts, lifestyle, amusements, and anything else people create that transcends their basic animal needs. The point of the book is to demonstrate that the multi-faceted popular culture of present-day Japan is an outgrowth of the culture generated not by aristocrats, samurai, or peasants but by the urban masses of the Edo period.

People around the world have eagerly embraced such items of Japanese popular culture as *karaoke*, instant noodles, and hot-tubs without any sense of the society from which they arose. At the same time, the word "Japanese" can conjure up feelings ranging from unreserved admiration to mistrust, resentment, and even fear. I believe this book, with its intimate linking of past and present, and its focus on ordinary people, will help lift Japan out of the realm of inscrutability. And for "old Japan hands," whose areas of interest tend to be limited, the potpourri of topics ensures many new discoveries. If you have cherished—or had problems with—some things Japanese without knowing how or why they came about, you may find the answers in this book.

Miriam Eguchi
Kobe, Japan

JAPANESE HISTORICAL PERIODS

- JOMON PERIOD (ca. 10,000 B.C.E.–ca 300 B.C.E.)
- YAYOI PERIOD (ca. 300 B.C.E.–ca 300 C.E.)
- KOFUN PERIOD (ca. 300–552)

Hunting and gathering gives way to sedentary agricultural-based life and village settlements.

- ASUKA PERIOD (552–645)

Influx of Chinese culture (Buddhism, writing system, Confucianism, religious Taoism, calendar, etc.).

- NARA PERIOD (646–794)

First permanent capital at Nara; rising refinement of life at imperial court and among nobility; first Japanese writings, including Shinto mythologies and dynastic chronicles.

- HEIAN PERIOD (794–1185)

Kyoto becomes capital; life among court and nobility becomes increasingly sophisticated; warrior class rises to power.

- KAMAKURA PERIOD (1185–1333)

Political power shifts from aristocracy to warrior leaders; military dictator settles in Kamakura (emperor is isolated at Kyoto); emergence of merchant class; growing instability; development of popular Buddhist sects.

- MUROMACHI PERIOD (1333–1568)
- MOMOYAMA PERIOD (1568–1600)
- WARRING STATES PERIOD (1482–1558)

Also Azuchi-Momoyama. Extended civil war; advancements in agricultural techniques; culture and sophistication of aristocracy trickle down and blend with culture of warrior class; Oda Nobunaga and Toyotomi Hideyoshi begin unification of country under military (to be completed by Tokugawa Ieyasu in early 1600s); growth of towns and cities; first major contacts with West.

- EDO PERIOD (1600–1867)

  Also called the Tokugawa period. With establishment of Tokugawa shogunate by Tokugawa Ieyasu, peace and stability reign; shogunate based in Edo (present-day Tokyo); "closed door" policy restricts foreign access to Japan; Christianity suppressed; rise of merchant class which dominates economic and cultural affairs; rapid expansion of popular arts among the masses.

- MEIJI ERA (1868–1911)
- TAISHO ERA (1912–25)
- SHOWA ERA (1926–89)
- HEISEI ERA (1989–   )

  Meiji Restoration of 1867 topples lethargic Tokugawa shogunate; emperor's authority restored; transition from feudal to modern period; feudal, military-dominated state gives way to modern nation-state based in Tokyo; rapid modernization and industrialization; ban on Christianity lifted; after World War II, democratic political system established; Japan becomes major economic power.

I

LEISURE AND RECREATION

The "Floating World" of the Public Bathhouse

Shin'ya Hashizume

> One of the best loved minor pleasures of the body in Japan is the hot bath. For the poorest rice farmer and the meanest servant, just as much as for the rich aristocrat, the daily soak in superlatively heated water is a part of the routine of every late afternoon.... They value the daily bath for cleanliness' sake as Americans do, but they add to this value a fine art of passive indulgence which is hard to duplicate in the bathing habits of the rest of the world.
>
> —Ruth Benedict,
> *The Chrysanthemum and the Sword*, Tuttle, 1954

The sense of what constitutes cleanliness varies widely from one ethnic group to another. Ask Masumi Ikeguchi, a counselor to university students from abroad. Her book *Ryūgakusei Nihon fushigi taiken* (Strange experiences of foreign students in Japan; TOTO, 1990) is a unique cross-cultural study in the form of conversations with students from various countries on their first-hand perceptions of Japan. Their single most common complaint was of cultural friction related to bathing.

To these students, the Japanese-style bath represented an encounter with the unknown. Those from Western countries in particular had been accustomed to washing themselves inside the tub, then sending the dirty water down the drain. In Japan, where you wash and rinse off *before* getting into the tub to soak, it is customary for several people to use the same bath water, together or in turn. Foreigners in Japan differ in their opinions as to which of the two methods is more hygienic. (Many Japanese, on the other hand, are shocked to learn that in Western countries the bath and toilet are located in the same room.)

One topic that arises again and again in foreigners' accounts of Japan is the observation that the Japanese are a bath-loving people. Certainly few other ethnic groups take as much pleasure in bathing as the Japanese, who might be said to rank with the ancient Romans in their enjoyment of this activity.

Any discussion of Japanese bathing really has to start with the development of the public bathhouse, or *furoya*. At the modern-day furoya everyone—regardless of social class—strips naked and gets into the same tub. This is a mass-culture phenomenon unique to Japan. For foreign visitors it is a source of perpetual amazement.

Until the early Edo period, even the Japanese took loincloths or wraparound waist cloths with them to the furoya to wear in the water as covering after a sort. Bathing fully naked is a comparatively recent custom.

Establishments similar to the Japanese furoya can be found in Korea and some parts of China, but most are saunas or steam baths, which are quite different from the Japanese hot-water baths.

Most Japanese associate furoya with imposing frontal exteriors resembling temple architecture. Nowadays, however, inconspicuous furoya utilizing the ground floors of modern buildings are on the increase in urban areas. As cities grow skyward, even the tall furoya chimneys, which once stood out as landmarks, tend to become lost between high-rise buildings. Sometimes the only thing that marks the presence of a furoya is the *noren* (sign curtain) imprinted with the words *yu* (hot water) or *o-furoya-san*, hanging at the entrance.

People arriving to bathe push aside the noren to step into the vestibule, take off their shoes, then proceed into the bathing area through different entrances for men and women. Between the two entrances is a watcher's seat, where the entry fee is paid.

At present the men's and women's sections are clearly separated by a wall, but in the past it was common for people of both sexes to bathe together. Beginning in the late eighteenth century, the authorities issued a series of edicts prohibiting mixed bathing—inspired, perhaps, by frequent indecent occurrences.

These were of only questionable effectiveness, however, for men's and women's bathing areas did not become completely separate until the Meiji era, almost a hundred years later. At that time the government, self-conscious under the curious gaze of foreigners, began to close down any public baths that did not partition men's and women's facilities.

The dressing room at a modern-day furoya is equipped with a large mirror and rows of clothes lockers. There are also scales, massage machines, and hair dryers. The walls are adorned with posters announcing the latest plays and movies, invitations to join the Self-Defense Forces, advertisements for neighborhood businesses, and sometimes even wanted posters of criminals and missing persons.

Beyond the dressing room is the bathing area, a high-ceilinged space with a centrally located window that provides light and ventilation. The tub is in the middle, and the faucets where customers scrub down are spaced evenly out along the surrounding walls.

The Japanese furoya started out as a communal facility based on concepts of rationality and economy, but has performed other

Modern bathhouse with individual showers, large soaking tub (*rear, left*), and sauna (*rear, right*).

functions too. As suggested by the expression *hadaka no tsukiai* (socializing in the nude), chatting while soaking naked in a tub with others was once an indispensable part of neighborhood life. At the furoya people discussed everything from the pettiest local gossip to social conditions and political matters. This was where they introduced their new babies to the neighbors, and where newcomers to the area got to know people. Thus the furoya was not merely a public bath, but a community social space where people in towns and cities could exchange information and solidify their relationships. It is not surprising, then, that until the late fifties, when bathtubs in the home became the norm, there were furoya in every single neighborhood and community in Japan.

Now that almost everyone can bathe at home, public baths no longer attract the crowds they once did, but they still turn a brisk trade. When people want to relax and unwind after a long day's work, they sometimes head for the simple local furoya, or one of the updated versions equipped with *karaoke* corners, bars, meeting rooms, and refreshment areas. The place of the furoya in Japan has often been likened to that of the café in France and the pub in England. These, I think, are valid comparisons.

+   +   +

In very ancient times the custom of bathing in hot water did not exist in Japan. Instead, people cleaned their bodies by pouring cold water over themselves. Immersion was a custom that came to Japan via China and Korea in the seventh century, when it was introduced with Buddhism.

Because it was then believed that bathing cured illness and brought general well-being, all the ancient temples were equipped with baths. Several even opened these facilities to worshippers. Temple baths served a quasi-medical role, then, while at the same time helping to popularize the new religious beliefs.

Through their experience with temple baths the Japanese soon learned to appreciate the pleasure of immersing themselves in water. In the late Kamakura period, communal baths appeared that could be considered the predecessors of today's furoya. The earliest known example was a public bathhouse established within the precincts of the Gion Shrine in Kyoto.

The Muromachi period saw the birth of public bathhouses that took the names of streets or intersections, such as Gojō-Muromachi-buro and Ichijō-Nishinotōin-buro. These started to spring up in virtually every neighborhood, and so came to be called *machi-buro* (neighborhood baths). In those days, however, baths were heated with steam, rather than the hot water used today.

The machi-buro shown in illustrated Kyoto city maps of the Muromachi period were almost indistinguishable on the outside from ordinary houses in the town. The only noticeable difference was that the steam rooms had the decorative Chinese-style *karahafu* gables typical of temple architecture. This feature suggests to us that the bath still retained some religious overtones.

In the machi-buro of those times a bather's social class was not important; it was a matter of course for everyone to get into the same water. The Buddhist sense of equality seems to have prevailed in this situation. The lounge provided a space where people could socialize without regard for class or profession. There is even an anecdote about how soldiers on opposite sides in the civil war between the North and South Dynasties would battle each other during the day, and then bathe together at the same bathhouse in the evening. In this sense the machi-buro served as a sort of sanctuary or sacred territory.

Machi-buro were also patronized by the aristocracy, which was then the ruling class. Groups of nobles would reserve the entire bathhouse, using the lounge for drinking or tea parties.

The intimate relationship between the Japanese and their *furoya* grew to maturity in the incubator of the long, peaceful Edo period. In the seventeenth century, when towns were developing throughout the country, a type of public bathhouse known as *yuna-buro* came into fashion. These establishments featured the services of beautiful female bath attendants called *yuna*, who soaped customers down during the daytime, and served them at drinking parties in the evening in party rooms on the second floor. For an extra charge, some yuna-buro apparently provided sexual services as well.

Because the yuna-buro presented a problem from the standpoint of public morality, they often became the target of official decrees. At first these were somewhat lenient, simply limiting the number of yuna to three per bathhouse. In 1657, however, yuna-buro were completely banned, and all the women sent to the Yoshiwara pleasure quarter.

The next kind of bathhouse to appear was the *ukiyo-buro* ("floating-world bath"), which differed from previous types in its ratio of hot water to steam. Hot water was now increased to 40 percent of the tub volume, resulting in a compromise between a steam and a hot-water bath. In all other respects, including the procedures for washing-up and bathing, the ukiyo-buro can be

Ukiyo-e print depicting typical women's bath. With male attendant at left. Print by Toyohara Kunichika, 1868.

viewed as the prototype of the present-day furoya. Someone then invented a way to construct the bathroom so as to prevent steam from escaping when people went in and out, and the amount of hot water in relation to tub volume was further increased, to 60 percent.

In the town of Edo, which tended to be windy and dusty, it was necessary to bathe every day. In those days, however, few people enjoyed the luxury of a bathtub in their own home. Some disadvantages of private bathing were inconvenient water facilities, the high cost of fuel necessary to heat the bath, and the danger of fire. Thus home bathing was uncommon until someone invented a practical home-use bathtub toward the end of the Edo period.

By the latter half of the nineteenth century every neighborhood in Japan's larger cities offered one or two furoya. Since people living in the same area saw each other at the bath every day, the furoya became an important channel for social intercourse. Its function as a place to exchange information was enhanced by the appearance at that time of illustrated sumo and theater posters on dressing-room walls.

+ + +

An interesting controversy concerning bathing customs in Japan revolves around the question of why there was a changeover from steam to hot-water baths. One factor that was certainly influential was the Japanese infatuation with hot springs. Japanese people customarily went off to mountain hot springs to recover from illness or injury. The belief in the curative powers of immersion in hot water was a kind of folk tradition that gradually found its way into neighborhood bathhouses.

It was not until comparatively modern times that furoya evolved into their present form, using only hot water. This transition was related to the "urban hot-spring" boom of the early Meiji era. The first of these facilities, featuring bathhouses with restaurants, was Hakone Shichi-yu (Seven Springs of Hakone), established in 1872 in Fukagawa, Tokyo. The "seven springs" were miniatures of hot springs in Hakone, a well-known mountain resort area south of Tokyo. Similar facilities soon sprang up one after another around the fringes of Tokyo and Osaka.

The water used in urban hot-spring baths obviously did not come from real hot springs gushing up in the middle of town. Rather, ordinary hot water was transformed into a medicinal bath by adding deposits collected from hot-spring sources elsewhere. Many bathhouses went even further, incorporating artificial waterfalls and other landscaping devices intended to re-create the scenery of particular hot-springs regions. In this way they sought to give the impression that they were the "local branches" of famous mountain resorts. Some establishments revived the second-floor party rooms of the former yuna-buro and provided attractive women to attend to customers at drinking parties.

The number of furoya in Tokyo tripled during the early Meiji era. The majority of the new establishments did not belong to the furoya guild or even have operating licenses, but had simply opened in the midst of the social confusion prevailing at the time. Most conspicuous were the urban hot springs described above, which attracted customers by offering food, drink, and medicinal baths. This competition could not help but influence the ordinary furoya, forcing them to make substantial changes.

First, the sixty-forty ratio of hot water to steam, the norm during the Edo period, now gave way to a regular hot-water bath system, with tubs filled to brimming. The new-style furoya were called "hot-spring baths" or "improved baths." Other improvements included higher ceilings and the addition of windows set higher up in the walls for better lighting and more efficient evacuation of steam. The bathrooms themselves were made brighter and more cheerful. In the Taisho era, painted murals of Mt. Fuji and the Matsushima islands began to appear on the bathroom walls. Their purpose was to incorporate the scenery of spa resorts into the interior of urban furoya.

After World War II, the concept of bathing in a resortlike setting underwent still further development. Beginning in the 1960s when almost every home had its own bathtub, it was the "variety bath" and "special bath" that helped keep the custom of public bathing alive. The "variety bath" is a type of furoya that provides all sorts of different facilities, including electric-current baths, baths to recline in, baths to sit in, open-air baths, medicinal baths, saunas, and shower massage. In other words, it is the "health spa around the corner." The still more ambitious "special bath" has a bar, a karaoke corner, a restaurant, and rooms for private parties. In effect, both kinds of modern furoya offer city dwellers a spa resort experience on an everyday basis, right in town.

+ + +

The Buddhist sense of equality combined with the pleasures of a hot spring—this, I think, forms the essence of the Japanese furoya. But why has it survived in modern Japan?

I think the answer lies in the concept of *ukiyo*, a sense of the value in momentary pleasure, that has been passed down from premodern times to the present day. This, I believe, is what lay behind the process whereby the passive pleasure of hot spring bathing made its way into city life.

Ukiyo, literally "floating world," symbolized a consciousness that permeated Japan's urban masses from the second half of the seventeenth century. Simply stated, it was a sense of values that placed priority on enjoying the moment, in view of the fleeting, unpredictable nature of human life. The word "ukiyo" was already in existence as early as 1661, when it was used in the title of a book called *Ukiyo monogatari* (Ukiyo tale). The genre called *ukiyo-e* (ukiyo woodblock print) is said to have begun with Hishikawa Moronobu in 1672, while Ihara Saikaku's best-selling novel *Kōshoku ichidai onna* (1686; translated as *The Life of an Amorous Woman*, 1963) prompted a boom in ukiyo books.

"Ukiyo" was embraced as a key word because it expressed the general inclination to pursue momentary enjoyment as an escape from the hardships and stress of everyday life. One such momentary pleasure was a soak in a hot bath.

I suspect that with daily bathing the spirit of ukiyo sank deep into the collective consciousness of the Japanese urban populace, and has been transmitted through the generations to the present day. Our own silhouettes in the mists of the furoya bear witness to this inheritance.

Why You Can't Have Green Tea in a Japanese Coffee Shop

Yasuo Takahashi

In every society, drinking with others is recognized as a way of facilitating communication and building relationships. The most obvious example that comes to mind in this connection is alcohol—yet drinking anything, even plain water, with others can help people attain a greater sense of harmony and kinship.

The most popular nonalcoholic "luxury beverages" throughout the world are coffee, tea, and cocoa. The popularization of coffee in the Islamic world and tea in the Buddhist world share a common background. Both religious traditions had doctrines banning the use of alcohol, with the result that people turned instead to stimulating beverages containing large amounts of caffeine. These drinks can function—almost as easily—as a glue and lubricant in human relations. It is not hard to understand why establishments that serve them, including coffee shops, cafés, teahouses, tea shops, chocolate houses, and coffeehouses have flourished in cities everywhere.

It should be noted that present-day Japanese *kissaten*, literally "tea shops", are actually coffee shops that serve various beverages, snacks, and light meals. With certain rare exceptions, they do not offer Japanese green tea. In modern Japan, just about the only eating or drinking establishments that serve green tea are Japanese-style restaurants and certain types of tea shops located in tourist areas. When we say, "Let's go have a cup of tea," the word "tea" most often refers to coffee! In this sense, the term "kissaten" itself stands as an interesting example of the way modern customs have grown away from traditional practices.

THE BIRTH OF COFFEEHOUSES

The custom of drinking coffee first took hold among the people of the Islamic world around the middle of the fifteenth century. Coffee was served at roadside stands set up in front of mosques, where worshippers commonly stopped in before the service. The world's first real coffeehouse, called Kafve Kanes, was opened in the Turkish city of Constantinople, present-day Istanbul, in 1554.

Coffee was transmitted to Europe in the seventeenth century. In 1615 the first coffee shop opened in Venice, which was at the time engaged in trade with Arabia. Shops next appeared in Paris in 1645, Oxford in 1650, and London in 1652. This kind of establishment sometimes became the object of political repression, but nevertheless continued to multiply. By the eighteenth century, there were said to be two or three thousand coffeehouses in London and six hundred cafés in Paris. Tea shops appeared around the same time.

These spaces brought together people from the worlds of literature, the arts, finance, and politics, giving rise to all kinds of new ideas and art forms. Out of the coffeehouses of Oxford and London, for example, came the Royal Society, Lloyd's, and various magazines and newspapers, while the Encyclopaedists were among the products of the Paris café scene. In this way, coffeehouses and cafés became matrices for the creation of modern urban culture.

CHAYA: THE WORLD'S FIRST TEAHOUSES

Tea was introduced into Japan with Buddhism back in the seventh century, but it was not until the fourteenth century that ordinary people had the opportunity to enjoy it. At that time a Kyoto business called *ippuku issen* ("one cup for one *sen*") turned a brisk trade selling tea to passers-by on the roadsides. By the beginning of the fifteenth century, simple commercial teahouses called *chaya* had sprung up in front of the gates of such famous religious establishments as Tōji temple, and teahouses catering to ordinary city dwellers appeared on the streets of Kyoto. Japan was probably the first country in the world to have shops that served tea to the public.

The early appearance of teahouses in Japan was directly related to a drop in the price of tea. This factor was decisive in the popularization of tea-drinking, especially when tea became so cheap that a cup could be had for a single sen, the country's smallest unit of currency.

At that time Kyoto was one of the world's leading cities, with a population estimated at between one and two hundred thousand, and was rapidly evolving its own distinctive mass culture. The development of tea-drinking was part of this process. A number of expressions came into common usage to describe people who liked tea—*cha-suki* (refined tea-lover), *cha-nomi* (tea-drinker), and *cha-kurai* (tea-gulper). This last referred to people who would jump at any chance to drink tea without knowing anything about its quality. Far and away the largest group, tea-gulpers were the mainstay of popular tea culture.

Several features distinguished the Japanese teahouses of the middle ages from the coffeehouses of Arabia and Europe. The

Sophisticated *chaya* near shrine. To left of shop entrance are tea cups and kettle; to right, sweets. Painting by Ippitsusai Bunchō, active circa 1772–74.

Typical roadside teahouse along a country trail. Mid to late nineteenth century.

teahouses were much smaller, humbler structures, with earthen floors, a hearth in one corner, and a few stools for customers in another. Their limited size did not allow them to function as gathering places for large groups. They had no walls or doors in front, but opened straight onto the road, giving the impression they were almost part of it. While the English coffeehouse developed as an alternative to the tavern, it appears that the roots of Japanese teahouses lay not in establishments serving saké, but in the age-old custom of offering wayfarers a cup of water or tea and a place to rest.

The people of Kyoto did not go to teahouses only to sip tea, but also to chat and exchange information. Later on, teahouses began serving other refreshments, including dumplings, rice cakes, and saké. Some employed waitresses, or even courtesans, to keep customers company. Still others featured gambling. Rather than limiting themselves to selling tea at one sen a cup, teahouses began to develop into businesses providing various services. But because they sometimes functioned as meeting places for criminals and political dissidents, they were often the target of legal restrictions.

With the start of the Edo period came the advent of sprawling "mass cities," the largest being Edo (present-day Tokyo), Osaka, and Kyoto. With urbanization, a multitude of specialized teahouses emerged from the medieval prototype. To name just a few, there were "water," "restaurant," "erotic," "theater," and "sumo" teahouses. The water teahouses, which sometimes employed pretty girls to stand out front as a lure for customers, provided tea and a place to rest at the roadside or within the grounds of temples and shrines. Erotic teahouses, which employed courtesans, became venues for private gatherings. Restaurant teahouses, serving both food and drink, were closed-in spaces far removed from the roadways, and offered instead of stimulation a sense of retreat.

COFFEE SHOPS: A REFLECTION OF THE TIMES

There was no great difference between these various establishments and present-day Japanese-style restaurants, teahouses, and clubs. It was not until modern times, however, that Japanese versions of the European or Arabian coffeehouses appeared, allowing people of various classes and walks of life to mingle freely and talk over a cup of coffee or tea. Coffee-drinking in Japan began in the hotels of the foreign settlements, which increased its already exotic appeal. To the Japanese, coffee was a symbol of Western culture and modernity.

Shops that doubled as retailers of coffee beans began to appear in Tokyo and Kobe in the early years of the Meiji era. The first modern kissaten along the lines of the French literary café was opened in the form of a two-story building in Shitaya, Tokyo, in 1888. Called Ka-hhi Chakan, this establishment served not only coffee but beer and other Western and Japanese alcoholic beverages, as well as meals, bread, and cake. The price of a cup of coffee was one and a half sen, and café-au-lait cost two sen. No tea of any sort was served. The shop provided equipment for games such as cards, billiards, go, and shōgi, as well as books, magazines, and stationery.

Café-style coffee shops soared in popularity from the latter years of the Meiji era. In 1910, a shop called Maison Kōnosu (House of the swan's nest) opened in the Koami-chō district of Tokyo. Featuring strong, well-roasted coffee in the French style, it soon began to function as a "writers' den." In 1911, the painter Shōzo Matsuyama opened Café Printemps, the first coffee shop to use the word "café" in its name, in Kyōbashi, Tokyo. Its salon-like interior became a gathering place for artists, writers, and intellectuals. The menu included Western meals and alcoholic drinks; the coffee, a blend of mocha, Java, and Brazil, sold for fifteen sen a cup.

Next came Café Lion, famous for its pretty waitresses. This last attraction soon became a typical feature of cafés in general.

The establishments most directly responsible for the popularization of coffee were the "milk halls," where coffee was served at prices geared to students, laborers, and housewives. Milk halls reached the peak of their popularity in the 1910s and 1920s. They provided newspapers and magazines, and served coffee in a cup the size of a beer mug for a modest five sen.

The twenties also brought a wave of diversification, as the shops competed for customers by introducing special features. This led to the emergence of coffee shops called "kissaten," with their multiplicity of features and sales points. Some kissaten were run by confectioners, who vied with one another to offer the most delicious and unusual pastries, and coffees originating in different Western countries. It was also around this time that *meikyoku kissaten* ("great-music coffee shops") came on the scene. Here, by paying ten to fifteen sen (two or three times the usual price) for a cup of coffee, a customer could enjoy a conversation with a well-bred young woman to the accompaniment of classical music. As the idea of "free love" grew in popularity, some coffee shops began to emphasize the services and erotic dress—or lack of it— of waitresses as sales points.

THE POLARIZATION OF COFFEE AND GREEN TEA

Throughout this century, the relationship between coffee and green tea in Japan has been one of the new to the old, with a nuance of rivalry between modern and traditional, or Western and Japanese culture. For example, once coffee-drinking caught on among the general public, it was not long before the water teahouses were superseded by the kissaten. Now the former can be found only at certain famous historical spots.

A modern coffee shop. A sense of intimacy is reinforced by soft wood surfaces and the master's presence.

Here the story becomes somewhat more complex. People tend to think in terms of the intellectuality of Tokyo and the more popular character of Osaka; but as Osaka cafés advanced into Tokyo, brandishing their explicit sexuality, the literary and artistic atmosphere of Tokyo's cafés gradually dissipated. Soon these too were following the Osaka example, taking on more and more of the flavor of a new "sex business." This development propelled them into competition with that older variant on the erotic theme, the teahouse, with its tradition reaching back several hundred years. The merits and demerits of the geisha teahouse versus the "waitress café" became a topic of earnest debate. Finally the cafés went on to become the postwar cabarets, while geisha teahouses remained unchanged.

Another aspect of the post–World War II scene is that the exterior and interior decor, menus, functions, and services of the kissaten ("kissa" for short) have undergone repeated transformations to reflect the changing social scene. Just a few of the variations that have appeared since the mid-1950s are *amatō* ("sweet-tooth") kissa; game kissa; music kissa (which can be subdivided into famous works, jazz, classical, rock, singing, go-go, mood, *karaoke*...); and shops with sexual nuances (parlor, beautiful-girl, social, no-panty, topless, private-room, and date kissa). While some of these have proved to be no more than passing fads, the way kissaten keep changing from year to year and generation to generation can be likened to a mirror reflecting the mores and customs of the times.

KISSATEN AND THE NEW GENERATION

Since the 1980s, the custom of frequenting ordinary kissaten has been waning among young people, as evidenced by a steady decrease in the number of shops. The diffusion of fast-food outlets has been pointed out as one reason for this decline. Another contributing factor was the lifting of import restrictions on coffee in 1960 and on instant coffee the following year. As a result, coffee came to be widely used at home as an alternative to green tea. Coffee had finally completed its transformation from an exotic luxury into a plain, everyday commodity. Finally, wide improvements to the kind of homes people live in has meant that the kissaten is no longer indispensable as a substitute for a living or drawing room, or a place to conduct business discussions. The role of the kissaten in providing an "interface" for exchange of information may be becoming redundant in today's modern city.

The dizzying, kaleidoscopic changes made by the kissaten can be said to reflect its desperation to survive. These days, the kissaten's appeal depends on the extent to which it provides a novel kind of space and up-to-the-minute information. In its perpetual transformations we can actually glimpse the shifting face of Japan as an "information society."

Two types of kissaten that have gained popularity recently are the café-bars (bars that serve coffee), and shops with a lively, open atmosphere that fits in well with the general downtown scene. In addition to coffee, the beverage menus of most kissaten now include imported black teas with milk or lemon, as well as juice and soft drinks—but you still can't order a cup of green tea.

The kissaten culture in Japan may be at the threshold of a new phase involving a return to some of the original forms: the London coffeehouse, the Parisian café, the Kyoto teahouse. On the other hand, it is equally possible that in the near future the only remnants of kissaten will be a scattering of clubs for nostalgic, middle-aged coffee and tea lovers.

Pachinko: The Lonely Casino

Tsutomu Hayama

One television commercial opens with the slogan, "Businessmen! Can you keep up the fight twenty-four hours a day?" Keeping busy has long been associated with virtue in Japan. White-collar workers, in particular, have gained a reputation as "workaholics"—and for the most part the epithet is entirely appropriate.

From the postwar period of rapid economic growth through the present "information age," the pinball game known as *pachinko* has provided an everyday recreational outlet for Japan's harried working population. Of all the leisure industries with some relationship to gambling that have taken root in modern Japanese society, it has been by far the most successful.

Typical pachinko parlor.

The hard data shows pachinko to be a mammoth industry with annual proceeds amounting to about thirteen trillion yen, more than 4 percent of the Japanese gross national product. At last count there were approximately sixteen thousand pachinko parlors and three-and-a-half million pachinko machines in Japan, corresponding to one machine for every thirty-five citizens. Three million machines are manufactured each year. The number of regular players is estimated at about thirty million, and they are served by over four hundred thousand employees. The industry accounts for more than one-fifth of Japan's leisure market.

The prevalence of pachinko lovers in the nation was reflected in a survey of white-collar workers: 90 percent of respondents had indulged in this form of gambling at some point, as opposed to 70 percent for mah-jongg and 40 percent for horse racing.

There is a pachinko parlor in virtually every shopping district of every city in the nation, and even small train stations have at least one nearby. Pachinko is the single most popular form of recreation among the urban population of Japan. It would be a mistake to try to understand Japanese popular culture without considering the role of this omnipresent pastime.

+ + +

Pachinko is not very complicated: you just flip balls up to the top of a board and hope they will enter a series of holes as they make their way down again. Why has so simple a game enjoyed such great success, filling the cities to bursting with its establishments and holding the public in thrall? In the next few pages I shall try to account for pachinko's appeal, and describe how it was made accessible to Japan's urban populace.

Pachinko is played alone. It is rare for people to visit pachinko parlors in groups. Unlike many sports, this game is not broadcast on television, and no space is provided for spectators to watch the players in their contest with the machines. It is strictly the customer against the machine.

The amount of space allotted to each player is extremely small, but no one ever complains about the cramped playing conditions. Japanese are accustomed to a confined space, as evidenced by crowded residential areas and jam-packed commuter trains. Even when they are practically stuck together in the physical sense, it has become second nature to erect invisible walls of consciousness around themselves. In fact, being crowded together in a small space almost seems to give them a sense of security.

At the pachinko parlor they sit in front of the pachinko machine, absorbed and fascinated, as they concentrate their full attention on the movement of the shiny steel balls cascading over pins. The movement and sound are diverting and enable players to experience a blank state of mind and enjoy a sense of detachment, completely heedless of their surroundings.

Pachinko involves a strong element of chance. The game has its experts, of course, who achieve consistently good results, but for the ordinary public, who cannot spend all their time in pachinko parlors mastering the game, the movements of the balls are largely unpredictable. Indeed, for the average player the balls seem to move about as capriciously as fish in an aquarium, and at infinitely more dizzying speeds.

Now that the lever that flips up the balls has become electronic rather than manual, the player no longer needs to operate it for each play. This development has increased the element of chance even more. Whether or not a ball enters a hole now depends mainly on the positions of the nails, which act as deflectors. Since the layout of the nails is different for each machine, getting a good one is a matter of luck. As a game that deliberately incorporates the element of chance and offers prizes in exchange for balls accumulated, pachinko must be defined as a form of gambling—one of the few officially recognized in Japan.

The unique exterior and interior of pachinko parlors is, for many, another part of their charm. Outside, they proclaim their existence with enormous garlands of plastic flowers and bright lights that flash night and day. Inside, there is clamor, lively music, brilliant lighting, and still more gaudy decor. The whole effect is of a humming, pulsating place, far removed from the humdrum realities of everyday life.

Finally, it is easy to play pachinko. The action is simple, consisting merely of flipping up the balls. Since the outcome is decided in a matter of seconds, even someone with just a few minutes of spare time can drop in for a moment of relaxation and fun. It is also convenient; parlors are everywhere, in handy locations, and the price of one round is only a hundred yen. Pachinko is a "roadside recreation" that can be enjoyed by anybody, anywhere, anytime.

+ + +

Pachinko began with the seminal idea of standing a Corinthian Game board upright. It uses a box-shaped vertical board with glass surfaces, and small steel balls that are flipped upward by a spring. Its rules are simple: if a descending ball goes into one of the holes, the machine spits out several more balls, and these can either be circulated back into play or exchanged for prizes.

The origins of pachinko are somewhat unclear. It is said to have begun when the Corinthian Game, the predecessor of the American pinball machine, was imported to Japan. Soon afterward, some manufacturer in Osaka or Kanazawa apparently came up with the idea of producing it in a vertical form to economize on space. A game that could be considered the prototype of present-day pachinko existed as far back as the twenties, when it was featured at fairs and in game corners of department stores. It was called *pachi-pachi* in Kansai (western Japan), and *gachanko* in the Tokyo region.

From that time on, pachinko has held onto its status as a recreational favorite despite a series of ups and downs. Because it falls into the category of an "industry affecting public morals," it has often been the object of government control. The game was completely prohibited during the years of the Pacific War, but was revived in 1945 when forms of public recreation were scarce. After that, a succession of improvements lent impetus to the growth in the game's popularity year by year. In 1952, for example, the "machine-gun model" appeared, which flipped balls up in rapid succession. Now the balls were supplied automatically with a flick of the lever, whereas previously they had to be inserted by hand one at a time. With the old machines, a semi-professional player could play up to a hundred balls a minute, the same time it took an ordinary player to do about thirty. The machine-gun model eliminated this gap, making the game even more appealing to the general public. The higher speed and increased gambling element of the new system, combined with other improvements, led to a tremendous boom. By 1953 the number of pachinko parlors had increased to a record high of about 45,000.

About this time the authorities must have decided that "pachinko fever" was heating up too much, because in 1955 they banned the use of the continuous shooting system. In their eyes, the use of a machine that allowed balls to be consumed at such high speeds led to overspending that exceeded the bounds of the "small-scale gambling" they considered acceptable. The ban put a temporary brake on the upsurge in pachinko's popularity, and there was a sharp decrease in the number of establishments.

A new machine appeared in 1957, designed to lure the public back to pachinko. It featured devices to enhance the visual appeal of the board by giving it greater variety and movement. This was one of the many attempts to make the game more interesting.

Although it suffered numerous setbacks as a result of official controls, the pachinko industry grew back each time like a weed, gradually increasing in strength. In the late 1960s the continuous shooting device was revived, and chairs were added to allow patrons to play sitting down, which encouraged them to relax and linger over the game. The next development was the transition from manual to electronic operation. While the old system of flipping up the balls had called for a certain amount of manual dexterity, the new electronically powered system enabled everyone, regardless of age, sex, or experience, to play on the same terms, thus widening the range of pachinko fans. This was the beginning of the large-scale incorporation of electronics into the game industry.

During the 1970s pachinko fell into another slump caused by a combination of factors including the oil shock, the rising popularity of video games, and a badly timed price raise. Frantic competition among pachinko parlors for customers forced proprietors to renovate every three months or so, a situation unheard of in any other industry.

Once again, however, the industry made a dramatic come-back—with the introduction of digital pachinko in 1980. The new "Fever Model," which used integrated circuits, was a combination pachinko and slot machine. When a ball entered a hole, it activated an internal slot machine. If you hit the jackpot, a huge number of balls would come cascading out.

This new machine had a particularly strong gambling element. It was greeted enthusiastically by the public, who enjoyed its heady, intoxicating quality, but it became the object of one regulation after another on the grounds that it encouraged too much gambling and speculation.

A rough sketch of pachinko's postwar history reveals a repeating cycle. First there is a shift from recreation to gambling, generating a boom; this becomes a social problem resulting in regulation, which causes a slump; then, in the midst of the slump, a new model is developed to revive the market. This pattern has occurred over and over again up to the present day. It represents a typical tug-of-war between a commercial enterprise pursuing profit and authorities seeking to maintain public order.

We could even say it corresponds to a tug-of-war between greed and conscience in the pachinko fans themselves. This repeating cycle enables players to indulge in a bit of gambling, satisfying their speculative spirit while assuaging fears of addiction.

+ + +

The development of pachinko machines over the decades has been a painstaking, step-by-step process involving the most advanced industrial technology. Not only have innovations in methods of operation emerged one after another, but there have been ongoing improvements in materials and structure. To mention just a few examples, the plywood base is constantly being made more moisture-resistant; the high-strength nails, driven five centimeters into the board, can now be hit several million times without loosening; double glass has been introduced to offset the effects of magnetic force; and balls are currently made of tempered steel to increase precision and prevent defacement. The subtle 13.6-millimeter tilt of the board, too, was arrived at only after years of trial and error.

There have also been operational improvements. These have included automatic ball-supplying devices, ball-dispensing machines, and ball-cleaning devices.

Incidentally, the man who invented an automatic ball-supplying apparatus called "octopus legs" apparently worked for Mitsubishi Aircraft as a draftee during World War II. He has been quoted as saying that the techniques he picked up there were later useful in developing the ball-supplier. This can be thought of as an example of the peaceful use of wartime technology.

Probably the most dramatic advances have come from the field of electronics. At present each machine incorporates twenty-one integrated circuits (ICs), including one large-scale integrated circuit (LSI). The number of prize balls distributed, as well as the

Pachinko machine.

probability of wins, are all controlled by computer. Thus most of the work formerly done by "nail specialists," who realigned the nails to control the movement of the balls, has now been taken over by LSIs. In other words the LSI, used in America for military equipment, is used in Japan for recreation.

The history of pachinko has been one of technology—with the pachinko machine embodying the most up-to-the-minute techniques available at any point in time. But the human element should not be overlooked, either. If not for several generations of entrepreneurs and inventors, pachinko would not be around today. The industry's continuing prosperity has grown out of the tireless pursuit of ideas to make the game more interesting, technical innovations to realize these ideas, and labor-saving devices to rationalize operations.

+   +   +

Pachinko is not the first roadside recreation to achieve popularity in Japan. One older game, called *hōbiki*, was originally an outgrowth and simplification of a traditional card game. As a form of gambling, hōbiki had existed since the Muromachi period, but it

Hana-fuda, an early card game of the common people.

flourished during the Edo period on bustling city streets as *tsuji-hōbiki*, or roadside gambling. It consisted of selling lots to a large number of people on a certain day, deciding the winning lots in a draw, and awarding winners large sums of money as prizes.

This practice, which lives on today in the form of lotteries, has a number of characteristics in common with pachinko. It involves an element of trusting one's fate to the heavens; the winnings may be converted into cash; and it is a characteristically urban form of gambling offered on roadsides where a great number of people come and go. Like pachinko, the low cost per unit of play enables people to choose how much money they want to wager. But most important, it is a form of gambling that may be indulged in alone.

Pachinko parlors today are trying to cultivate a bright, healthy image. With their hotel-style front desks, high-profile locations in shopping districts, and charming female attendants, they reflect the eagerness of the industry to target a wide clientele among both sexes.

There is every reason to think pachinko will continue to change with the times, and maintain its popularity as a convenient, inexpensive form of recreation that anyone can enjoy.

The Lesson Culture

Takeshi Moriya

Almost all Japanese, at some time in their lives, take nonacademic courses of one kind or another. They do this to better themselves culturally, or simply for enjoyment. This has fueled a tradition that could be termed "the lesson culture."

Collectively, the courses are called *o-keiko-goto*, and many of them fall into the category of traditional arts. In Japan the teaching of these has been dominated by a number of "schools," each run by a particular family (often the founding family). This family, or, more usually, the head of it, is called the *iemoto*. Often the school takes the form of an elaborate and wide-reaching "iemoto system," centered on the iemoto.

What exactly is the iemoto system? I would define it as an organization offering lessons of some kind and maintaining a body of instructors. Students enroll to follow a set, uniform curriculum. As they complete the various levels of this curriculum, they are issued progress certificates, for which they pay a fee. The instructors keep a percentage of this, passing the rest along up to the iemoto. To function effectively, therefore, the system requires a large hierarchy of instructors and students, with the iemoto at the top of the pyramid.

The iemoto system is a historical institution, yet it is also a very modern one that is flourishing to an unprecedented degree in the present day. This becomes apparent when the annual lists of people paying extremely high income tax are published—the names of several iemoto always figure prominently.

At one time some people could be heard saying that the iemoto system was a holdover from feudalism, and that its prevalence was a sign of Japan's backwardness. It is clear now, however, that this opinion was off the mark. The more modern society becomes, the more this system seems to gain in vigor and scope.

Another theory sees the iemoto system as the supreme illustration of uniquely Japanese human relations, and uses "iemoto" as a keyword for the distinctiveness of Japanese society. It would require a very thorough comparative study, however, to determine whether or not this type of organization is, in fact, peculiar to Japan.

One thing we do know is that the iemoto system did not exist in Japan from ancient times. It passed through its preparatory phases in the town society of the seventeenth century and was perfected in the eighteenth century. Not until the second half of the eighteenth century did the expression "iemoto" become widely used.

The courses first taught were tea ceremony, flower arrangement, and traditional performing arts such as dance. From the nineteenth century on, these were joined by various other artistic forms. Some iemoto organizations grew to span the entire country, while others targeted specific regions.

✛ ✛ ✛

O-keiko-goto is strictly a form of general education, or "education for the masses," and is quite different in character from education geared to training professionals. The iemoto system must therefore be considered in the context of how it accommodates the general public which supports it.

Central to the history of o-keiko-goto is the role played by the townspeople of the late seventeenth century. The prosperity of their cities made it possible for the lower middle classes of that period to accumulate wealth and create leisure time for themselves by taking advantage of flexible working hours. As a result, large numbers of them turned to o-keiko-goto. Their lessons were clearly a form of recreation, as indicated by another term given to the courses—*yūgei*, or "recreational arts."

"Arts" did not always refer to aesthetic disciplines such as singing and dancing. For the people of the Edo period, even lessons in medicine and gardening came under the heading of "yūgei." Anything and everything could be taught as o-keiko-goto, provided it was kept at the level of recreation. This tendency has much in common with attitudes today: for modern Japanese, pursuits such as language study and cooking have all turned into o-keiko-goto.

The emergence of the o-keiko-goto populace gave professional artists an alternative to the classical path of "seeking the Way." The new option might be called "teaching the art." It was the life of the "lesson-pro," sustained by the heightened interest in o-keiko-goto among the common city people. These circumstances led to a proliferation of local instructors, called *machi-no-shisho*, who specialized in "teaching the art" to amateurs. It was not essential that they be masters of their art—only that they be able to teach.

In the late seventeenth century city guides began to contain lists of local instructors, a practice that stimulated some people to turn to teaching, and others to seek them out. The activities of the instructors themselves also boosted enrollments in the o-keiko-goto. Like the proverbial chicken and egg, it is difficult to say whether the increase in instructors brought about the increase in students, or vice versa.

As time went on, recreational arts instruction entered a phase of systematization, as local instructors sought to be authorized by iemoto organizations. For the instructors, affiliation with a large, established school brought professional security by making it easier to attract students. From the standpoint of the school, taking an instructor into its system enabled it to absorb that instructor's students. The instructor could also be expected to recruit more students for the school in the future.

There is a similarity between this form of affiliation and the modern business practice of franchising. At the same time, the iemoto system functioned as a sort of teachers' trade union. It follows that when these organizations became widespread, it would have been difficult for teachers to make a living outside the powerful "union" if they broke away from their school.

The iemoto system placed the instructors in an intermediary position between the iemoto headquarters and the students.

Amateur students could also become instructors in their turn by completing the required curriculum. This is how iemoto in the past, as well as today, maintained an ongoing supply of capable intermediary instructors.

To develop a system of this kind, the iemoto had to meet social and institutional challenges such as establishing their own legitimacy and dealing with the feudal authorities. Internally, they were faced with the tasks of preparing curricula and converting the content of the art into a form that could be taught in a simple, enjoyable manner.

+ + +

Since the iemoto system is based on the principle of educating the general public—no one is excluded from it—we could say it has an open, democratic character. This is one of the reasons it currently enjoys the most prosperous period in its history, effectively absorbing today's rapidly growing numbers of o-keiko-goto students. Ultimately, the influence of a school is determined by the number of students it has, and the iemoto have a long history of appealing to many people from a wide variety of social backgrounds.

On the other hand, an essential element of the system is the importance of progress certificates, which the iemoto has the exclusive authority to issue. This monopoly assures the position of the hereditary iemoto at the top of the organization. In a sense, it is the source of the iemoto's status. The students can move up through the system, receiving certificates to mark their time and progress; but as long as they remain within the system, they can never attain the right to issue certificates themselves. They can never become the iemoto. In this sense, the organization is not democratic at all.

The only way to become an iemoto is to break away from the organization and start a new, independent school. The phenomenon of breakaway schools can occur at any time, and does in fact happen. There are no legal requirements for becoming an iemoto. This is a field of free competition.

It is difficult to predict, however, whether becoming an iemoto without an established reputation would actually be more advantageous than remaining in the original organization. For one thing, any promising individual who contemplates this move can anticipate some form of attack from the existing iemoto, who sense a threat to their vested interests. Historically, there are many examples of powerful iemoto harassing breakaway schools. From this standpoint, we would have to say that the iemoto system is extremely authoritarian and closed.

So the iemoto system is based on a dualistic principle: it is mass-oriented and open at the bottom, but authoritarian and closed at the top. Moreover, unlike regular academic schools, it offers no graduation ceremonies to release students from this dual structure. There is simply a point at which one cannot go any higher. The people who act as buffers to absorb the contradictions of this dual structure are the instructors, who often find themselves in the ambiguous position of being neither amateurs nor professionals.

+ + +

As a rule, o-keiko-goto is something one undertakes as an end in itself, rather than as a means to achieve some practical goal. It is considered inappropriate in Japan to think of art as something that might improve one's lot in life. Even if studying an art eventually does turn out to be useful in some way, that should not have been the intention from the beginning. In this sense, giving children piano lessons is a typical example of o-keiko-goto. No one begins piano lessons expecting to become a concert pianist.

The primary goal of o-keiko-goto, then, is nothing more than self-satisfaction; in the iemoto system this is embodied in progress certificates. Progress certificates are the key to the iemoto system. They are closely related to the mass-oriented, open nature of o-keiko-goto and the consciousness of the students who support the iemoto system from the bottom up. For the students, certificates provide the most tangible standard for measuring how much they have achieved in their study. By acquiring certificates at each level, from beginner to advanced, they experience a sense of their own progress and the satisfaction of achievement.

Since certificates imply evaluation, students naturally expect them to be backed up by a recognized authority. Understandably, they would rather receive a certificate from a famous iemoto than from one who is unknown. The greater the authority of the iemoto, the more valuable the certificate.

The iemoto, who are well aware of this, are under constant pressure to demonstrate their authority. One of the ways they do this is by making appearances from time to time to "Expound The Way." Although the day-to-day instruction in the iemoto system is quite practical, the utterances of the iemoto themselves always take the form of spiritual discourses reminiscent of what one might expect from the revered leader of a religious sect. It is no coincidence, either, that the publications issued by the iemoto are similar in tone to magazines published by religious organizations.

+ + +

While the Japanese have been taking all kinds of lessons since the Edo period, until recently the iemoto system was largely limited to teaching the traditional art forms. Now, however, iemoto systems, and organizations that could be called "quasi-iemoto systems," have become conspicuous in the newer artistic and musical fields as well. This is because people recognize the advantages of the pyramidal structure for attracting and "processing" students.

The issuing of progress certificates, or a substitute of some kind, is as much a factor in the new iemoto systems as in the old. Many people now take their lessons at so-called culture centers, which offer a wide selection of courses; instructors at these centers are normally supplied by certificate-issuing bodies. Not even a very famous artist would qualify to teach at a culture center without being a member of a recognized organization, because most people who take lessons expect to receive authorized certificates.

At culture centers you can attend classes in a variety of disciplines from flower arrangement and calligraphy to dressmaking, foreign languages, jazz dance, and just about anything anyone might want to learn. In other words, the centers have made an innovative leap—the gathering together under one roof of different types of o-keiko-goto that had formerly been taught only in separate schools or studios.

This development has brought new business opportunities to both the modern and traditional iemoto, who control the world of organized instruction. The structure of the culture center is similar to that of a department store in which boutique owners rent their premises: instructors are dispatched there from various schools, and set up their classrooms as "tenants."

Because there is a limit to what can be taught under these conditions, students who make a certain amount of progress are eventually invited to study at the instructor's private studio. After that, they are invited to "come to headquarters." In this way the culture centers have further strengthened the iemoto system by providing an effective means of recruiting new students.

As long as the number of o-keiko-goto students continues to increase, and they recognize the value of progress certificates, it is safe to assume that the iemoto of old and new fields alike will continue to glory in their prestige and prosperity. Recently, however, there are signs—albeit still quite faint—of a move away from progress certificates, especially among culture center students.

Iemoto for one of the ikebana schools.

Such people are proving to be not particularly attracted by the idea of moving up to the advanced levels.

"After all," they say, "it's only o-keiko-goto. We won't learn anything really difficult. What's the use of getting a certificate anyway?"—and as soon as they finish the basic course they form clubs among themselves, for enjoyment only.

At present, these people are still only a small minority. If the tendency becomes more pronounced, however, it could end by weakening the iemoto's base of authority and prestige. Although now enjoying the greatest popularity in its history, then, the iemoto system may actually be approaching a turning point critical to its future.

Package Tours, Pilgrimages, and Pleasure Trips

Akinori Kato

Tourism on a massive scale is a byproduct of peace. As soon as a society becomes fairly stable and affluent, there is likely to be an interest in travel. If coupled with assurances of convenience and safety, the idea of an overseas vacation is likely to become popular.

A vacation should include a certain amount of tension and excitement, but the overall experience should be safe and enjoyable. These criteria are met remarkably well by the package tour, the traveling style of choice for millions of Japanese every year, and as a result the package tour has played an important role in the development of Japan's postwar tourism industry.

The formal Japanese term for a package tour means "all-inclusive travel plan." By definition, it encompasses transportation, accommodation, and sightseeing arranged by an agent, then made available to the public as a standardized product. In this way, a large number of travelers can be sent out on tour after tour, while the planners need work out only a single itinerary.

From the consumer's point of view, package tours have many merits: Contents and costs are known in advance; there are no bothersome arrangements and paperwork; prices are generally reasonable; if problems occur, the travel agent or escort steps in to solve them; and in a land with a strange language, travelers can enjoy each other's company. With every detail taken care of by the escort and local personnel, even inexperienced travelers can enjoy a smooth, worry-free trip.

Naturally there are disadvantages too. A fixed itinerary makes it difficult to make changes or cancellations. The tour planners often try to crowd in too many attractions, resulting in a ludicrously tight schedule. Doing anything independently from the group or visiting out-of-the-way spots is next to impossible. Despite these drawbacks, however, Japan's package tour industry has expanded tremendously during the postwar period, especially in the area of overseas travel.

In April 1964, the year of the Tokyo Olympics, restrictions on overseas travel were lifted, and travelers were allowed to take the equivalent of five hundred U.S. dollars out of the country every year.

One hundred and twenty-eight thousand Japanese traveled abroad that year. Twenty-five years later, the figure passed the ten million mark, a phenomenal rate of growth. Undoubtedly the major factor for this growth was the proliferation of the package tour.

It is generally acknowledged that the first overseas package tour for Japanese was the Push-Button, introduced by Swissair in July 1964. The following year saw the debut of Japan Air Lines' Jalpack, which was to become synonymous with overseas travel. The first Jalpack tours were followed by a deluge of packages offered by competing airline companies.

In 1968 wholesalers entered the market, offering new package tours, and travel companies began to promote overseas tours themselves, taking over this role from the airlines. Then in 1970, the year of the World Exposition in Osaka, the industry received a powerful stimulus in the form of the new jumbo jet—which ushered in the concept of bulk fares based on bulk transport and sales. Now wholesalers could purchase tickets at a discount of 60 percent off the normal fare and reduce the prices of package tours accordingly.

This development heralded the popularization of overseas travel. In 1971 the number of Japanese traveling abroad topped one million for the first time, and the government enacted the New Travel Industry Law. Under this law travelers were clearly designated as consumers, which meant that travel agents could be held liable for the safety and rights of their customers. This farsighted law reassured the general public and opened the floodgates to massive tourism.

From 1972 on there was a travel boom, with the supply creating the demand. Tourism on a grand scale had arrived. There have been various setbacks since then, including the oil shock of 1973, and such notable improvements as the introduction of package tours using chartered flights in 1978. When companies started using newspaper advertisements to recruit customers in even greater numbers two years later, the package tour system was seen to have matured.

As of 1989 there were approximately five hundred types of overseas tours available in Japan, catering to about 60 percent of the ten million overseas travelers. A 1992 estimate revealed similar figures. The exclusion of those traveling on business yielded an even higher percentage: about 80 percent of the 11.7 million Japanese who traveled abroad listed nonbusiness reasons for traveling on their exit forms, and about 70 percent of these used package tours.

Not surprisingly, the package tour market has become more and more diversified, with the leading travel firms setting up alternative tours to appeal to different types of clients. There are tours for which the traveler selects the content; honeymoon or

Checking in for group tour.

deluxe types; tours with a large portion of free time; tours that allow the traveler to spend a leisurely holiday in one particular city or island; tours to little-known regions; gourmet tours; and theme tours planned around a particular hobby or interest. Some tours are aimed at specific age groups, such as trips for senior citizens with an accompanying medical doctor, and language-study tours for students. The people who sign up for these new types of holiday packages are often repeat travelers who want to try something different. For first-time travelers, the most reassuring option is still the classic "excursion tour" that whisks them around to various places with maximum economy of time and an ever-present escort.

+ + +

This standardized approach to travel, while valid within the Japanese social context, has become an object of ridicule abroad, reinforcing the impression that the Japanese can only function in a group, like sheep. Yet the custom is not simply a matter of groupism or a natural timidness, but traces its roots back to premodern times, when ordinary people from many walks of life began to make pilgrimages to the Grand Shrines of Ise in Mie Prefecture.

It is believed that the concept of individual recreation in Japan is a phenomenon of the modern age. In premodern times "recreation" was by definition a group affair, deriving its social acceptability from the general view that it was indulged in for the sake of the gods. In other words, activities that might normally be frowned upon as impractical and frivolous were condoned on the basis of their group-oriented, religious nature.

It makes sense, then, that popular travel in the Edo period consisted mainly of pilgrimages with an ostensibly religious purpose. Not only did these excursions to shrines and temples provide an opportunity for fellow travelers to get to know each other better, but the travel spirit permeated the whole village through such customs as send-off parties and bringing back souvenirs for those who stayed behind. There was also a recreational aspect to the pilgrimage that gave it the character of a sightseeing trip.

The pilgrimage to Ise was a typical example of popular travel. This holiest of shrines had originally been off-limits to commoners, but was opened to the public from about the middle of the Heian period. In response to the increase in visitors during the middle ages, shrine officials were obliged to establish a set of "spiritual rules" for paying homage at the shrine. The existence of detailed instructions concerning taboos and so forth showed that a growing number of ordinary people were visiting the sacred spot.

In medieval times there were many difficulties for individual travelers to overcome. They had to contend with social and political instability, barrier stations, and lack of accommodation. The complicated spiritual rules for shrine worship were an added deterrent. We can assume, therefore, that the most common form of shrine visit was the group pilgrimage, led by an experienced guide corresponding to the present-day tour escort.

The pilgrimages to Ise Shrine were supported by village associations. Since the sixteenth century, these associations had adopted a proxy system in which members made regular contributions to a fund that was used to send representatives to Ise. All long-standing members were assured of the opportunity to join a group pilgrimage at least once during their lifetime.

As these associations multiplied and flourished, they began to send young men on the pilgrimages—to give them, as future family heads, a chance to benefit from an educational experience. Thus travel took on the nuance of a training exercise. The pilgrimage came to function as a coming-of-age ceremony, and anyone who had not had the benefit of this experience was not treated as a fully-fledged adult.

As this practice spread, the act of paying homage at Ise became firmly established as a kind of civil obligation. On the other hand, many people, especially women and children, had neither the time nor money to join a regular excursion. People in this situation would sometimes sneak off without permission from their families, a practice called *nuke-mairi*. It was common also among apprentices and servants whose masters would not allow them to leave work.

The social attitude that developed around nuke-mairi dictated that people who ran away from their homes or masters for this purpose were not to be blamed or punished. It also became customary for wealthy persons to offer material aid to nuke-mairi pilgrims along the way.

By the time the Edo period came along, the practice of nuke-mairi had spawned another form of group pilgrimage called *okage-mairi*, perhaps best translated as "freeloading pilgrimage." As children, servants, and others too poor to join a regular pilgrimage traveled down the roadways, they attracted the attention of people living in the regions along the way. Before long, the ranks of the original pilgrims were swollen with spur-of-the-moment pilgrims who took advantage of the opportunity to tag along. And since residents living along the pilgrimage routes were obliged to offer substantial alms to pilgrims, as well as lodging, food, and other travel needs, it was a good chance to go on a trip without spending any money.

Needless to say, practices such as nuke-mairi and okage-mairi could not have emerged and spread as they did were it not for the

A "freeloading" group pilgrimage to Ise Shrine. Edo period.

deeply rooted religious faith connected with Ise Shrine, and the social consensus supporting this faith.

The pilgrims' traveling costume consisted of a white pilgrim's dress or sleeveless garment, a walking stick, a sedge hat, and a dipper slung from the waist. The native province and name of the pilgrim were written in large letters on the hat. With banners inscribed with the name of their association or decorated with ribald drawings, these pilgrims were a lively, eye-catching sight. Some groups made the pilgrimage in gaudy clothing, singing Ise chorus songs and acting as if the whole thing were a kind of parade.

Pilgrimages took on the air of a pleasure trip, and eventually a pleasure quarter called *ashi-arai-ba* developed in the Furuichi area between the Outer and Inner Shrines. People would set out on a trip using the pilgrimage as an excuse, go through the motions of praying at the shrine, and then spend the bulk of their trip in the pleasure quarter.

✛ ✛ ✛

As a social convention, the premodern pilgrimage to Ise was clothed in the garments of the collective value system, which disguised its true nature as a pleasure trip. Is this true of travel today?

I would say it is. Like the early pilgrimage, present-day Japanese group travel both abroad and inside Japan itself tends to have an educational or religious nuance that camouflages, or at least justifies, the recreational element. Two obvious examples of this in the domestic arena are school trips to places like Kyoto and Nara, and excursions to holy places.

All children attending Japanese schools go on group trips of two or more days in the last year of elementary, junior high, and high school, and often in between as well. Although the stated purpose of these trips is to "broaden their experience of society," most children look forward to them for months, and have a wonderful time. Like package tours in general, both the destinations and sightseeing objectives of school trips have been determined long before, and the same itinerary is used for successive groups year after year. There are countless regulations governing group conduct, but even when these become too strict and confining and students demand the privilege of helping to plan their own trips, the educational aspect is never discarded.

Modern-day pilgrimages to holy spots are popular among middle-aged women and older people of both sexes. Some itineraries are quite ambitious—for example, the well-known tour of eighty-eight Shingon Buddhist temples on the island of Shikoku. This may be done in one trip or divided up, and the amount of time it takes depends on whether or not a bus is used. During the day the pilgrims hike up and down mountainsides to pay homage at all the temples; but in the evening they relax at an inn, enjoying each other's company and the local culinary favorites.

Because these "contemporary pilgrims" often dress in white robes, and their rigorous schedules involve a good deal of walking and climbing, these trips can also be looked on as a form of physical and spiritual training. In fact, more emphasis seems to be placed on the process of moving around than on reaching the destination. Pilgrimages are highly regarded by Japanese society as much for the effort and perseverance involved in making them as for their religious implications.

Overseas package tours also tend to stress motion over content—and when taken to extremes, they too can resemble a rigorous training exercise. The recreational element is not entirely absent, certainly; but nuances of discipline and endurance may be very much in evidence as well, especially for people on their first trip abroad. Package tour participants put up with all kinds of things that would be unheard of on a truly recreational vacation. They may, for example, be permitted only momentary glimpses of famous attractions before being herded back onto the bus. Also common are fixed-menu meals for the whole group at restaurants, and lump purchases at elite boutiques.

Package tours are designed to provide an instant, compact "educational experience." People expect them to include all the famous sightseeing attractions of the places visited, and a smattering of cultural exposure in the form of dance, musical, or dramatic performances. Often the guide contributes a running narrative of historical and statistical information throughout the tour.

Ironically, a tourist is likely to learn more about a foreign country by traveling independently, exploring at leisure, and interacting with the local people. For package tour users, however, the important thing is having access to predetermined sightseeing and shopping opportunities with all the arrangements taken care of. Such tours usually involve a hectic itinerary and massive purchases of local products. In the process, the knowledge one gains of other countries is often superficial and standardized. As an introductory trip the package tour is adequate, yet many people fall into the trap of thinking they are now experts on the places they visited.

In the pilgrimage to Ise we could already discern certain features of the package tour: the group-and-leader element, the suggestion of a training exercise, and a festive, uninhibited atmosphere. Another thing these two types of group travel have in common is the great number of travelers they have attracted among the general population. I believe the reason for their overwhelming popularity is that Japanese society affirms the educational value of learning about the world. What we see here standing out in bold relief is the character of the Japanese, who cannot even go on a simple pleasure trip without choosing a socially approved form of travel.

Reconsidered in this light, the package tour format, with its guaranteed, standardized content, seems to offer one final benefit: it is a kind of "insurance" against disapproval in a society where everyone is expected to be doing something useful at all times. Participants can justify their indulgence in travel because society favors this travel option as the most efficient way to learn about foreign countries.

The Electric Geisha

Kunihiro Narumi

The Japanese tolerance for public exhibition of "hidden talents" at bars and parties may have its roots in the geisha party. The geisha profession began in the large cities of the Edo period. The role of the geisha at a traditional Japanese party was not so much to display her own talents as to act as facilitator—employing her skills to draw out the guests and help them have a good time together. For example, as she played the *shamisen*, a three-stringed banjo-like instrument, she encouraged guests to sing along. The art (*gei*) of the geisha was not so much performance-oriented as participatory. *Karaoke* can be thought of as a kind of "electric geisha," in the sense that it draws people together and helps them communicate.

The word *karaoke* is the abbreviation of an expression that translates literally as "empty orchestra": the recordings used in karaoke contain the instrumental tracks, while the vocals are provided on the spot by willing participants.

Karaoke first appeared around 1975, when it was introduced into bars in Japan's urban entertainment districts. At that time, bars leased the equipment from manufacturers. Soon after, karaoke sets were developed for home use, and they may now be found in many households. They are especially popular in rural areas, where entertainment and recreation opportunities are fewer than in urban settings.

When it was first developed, karaoke offered just simple cassette tapes, a microphone, and a songbook. The state-of-the-art version today uses laser discs. Each laser disc contains twenty-eight songs. Once a selection is made, the machine automatically searches for the desired track, like a jukebox. A television screen displays the lyrics superimposed over a short video clip designed

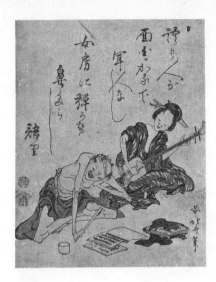

Wife accompanies husband's singing on *shamisen*. By Hokusai. Edo period.

to suit the mood of each song, making it that much more interesting for the listeners. Since the lyrics shown on the screen change color in time with the music, even an inexperienced performer can easily sing along with the karaoke music. The tempo and pitch are adjustable.

Let us consider the number and types of songs to be found in a karaoke set. One popular set contains 2,139 selections. Broken down by type, these include ten Hawaiian, five Christmas, thirty-four Korean, eleven military, and twenty-eight popular Western songs, with the remainder being Japanese tunes. This last category ranges from old standards (*natsu-mero*, or nostalgic melodies) to the hits of the latest pop idols; there are also 112 male-female duets.

✦ ✦ ✦

While karaoke can easily become an irritating source of noise pollution if misused, it has many positive aspects as well. For families who enjoy popular songs, singing together to karaoke accompaniment provides a good opportunity for relaxing together. It is also effective at parties. Unlike Western parties, where people usually entertain themselves with conversation and dancing, Japanese gatherings often slide into venues for guests to show off their

The old and the new: two "generations" of entertainment side by side—the geisha and the "electric geisha," or *karaoke*.

lesser-known talents. These might consist of magic tricks or other specialized performances, but there is almost always some singing.

People used to sing *a capella* at parties while listeners clapped along. Needless to say, not everyone could shine under such circumstances. But armed with karaoke's background music and voice-enhancing microphone, even people who are relative strangers to singing can give a reasonably good performance. Moreover, with thousands of selections available it is easy to find at least one familiar song.

Karaoke's appeal knows no national bounds. This was brought home to the participants in the New Town World Forum in Osaka in 1987. One evening after the program, the Japanese staff and a group of visitors from Germany and Holland went off to a bar to socialize. At first the guests felt somewhat lost, but when the Japanese started singing jazz standards and Beatles songs to karaoke accompaniment, a couple of the Europeans expressed a desire to try the sing-along machine. Before long, they were all singing "Lili Marleen" together.

In apartment complexes in German cities there is little sense of

Typical *karaoke* set-up (*above*) with music and lyrics accompanying short video clip (*left*).

community, and vandalism is rampant. When this problem was brought up at the forum, one of the Germans who had taken part in the round of karaoke expressed the opinion that a device of this nature would be useful for developing community spirit in her own country. "In a very short time, people who hardly knew one another were singing together," she said. "Singing can't help but bring people closer together." She added that she would like to buy a karaoke set to take home.

But karaoke does more than break down social barriers. It also lets people indulge in intoxicating self-expression. Further, vocalizing is in itself a proven stress-reliever, and when done melodiously it becomes even more effective.

The Japanese are often said to be timid and unable to assert themselves. One quick glimpse into a karaoke bar dispels that stereotype. What is it about karaoke that allows Japanese people to shed their inhibitions? Strangely enough, it seems the secret lies in the microphone—the magic wand that creates an atmosphere in which self-assertion is acceptable. When Japanese find themselves clutching a mike, their transformation is instantaneous. Shy young people prance around like pop idols, while their normally reserved elders croon away with the hammiest of gestures and facial expressions.

+ + +

People everywhere like to sing, but the manner in which they do it for enjoyment tends to differ somewhat from one ethnic group to another. In Germany, for instance, many local societies called *Verein* or *Zunft* have sprung up in various regions since the mid-nineteenth century. Predominant among these are choral societies. The traditional love of choral singing is typical of Germany, one of the great centers of Western classical music. Another contributing influence may have been the custom of singing hymns in churches.

Japan too has a history of choral singing that dates back to the Meiji era. But this is usually oriented toward public performance; in Japan, choral singing primarily for enjoyment has never really taken off as a form of recreation.

However, in larger Japanese cities beginning in about the seventeenth or eighteenth centuries, lessons in such "recreational arts" as singing ballads to the accompaniment of a shamisen were popular with the general public. These vocal displays were not group efforts like choral singing, but stressed individual accomplishment and were pursued diligently by the common people and members of the otherwise dignified samurai class alike.

A book of songs for shamisen, called *Shamisen kayō shūseisho*, was published in 1703. This was not simply a collection of popular and recreational songs, but a carefully classified anthology compiled, apparently, by blind professional musicians. It was followed by a flood of similar publications. These song books, containing not only traditional songs but new compositions, contributed greatly to the popularization of shamisen songs—

especially since the books were frequently updated and new works added. Support for the proliferation of these collections came from the *iemoto* system, the networks of teachers who, under a master of their particular style of study, popularized the art (for more information on the subject, see *The Lesson Culture*).

In earlier times, the skills revealed in party situations were often something the performer had been studying in secret. When these were "exposed" at a party everyone was impressed, or pretended to be. The present-day customs of addressing the pianist at a bar as *sensei* (teacher) and teasing people who excel at karaoke by asking, "How much tuition have you paid?" may well have originated in the lesson-taking tradition of the Edo period.

Even when display of skill is not the objective, people at parties often find themselves singing without any electronic aids. What sorts of songs do they choose?

For urban residents whose roots lie in disparate parts of the country, the first songs chosen are often hometown favorites. In Japan each region has its own folk songs, which in many cases have been polished and refined over a number of years in the entertainment or pleasure quarters. From the Meiji era on, the spread of Western popular music and the mechanization of farming diminished the role of folk singing in everyday life, but through the efforts of composers and songwriters many songs from this tradition were recorded and played on the radio. In this way the entire nation became familiar with the local color they expressed.

Out of this process grew a kind of communication: someone would sing a certain folk song, and listeners would assume the singer came from the part of the country where the song had originated.

Then there is the high school song. In prewar Japan, each school and each dormitory throughout the country had its own particular song. These were sung not only at athletic competitions between schools, but on the radio as well. At parties and other get-togethers, people often welcome the chance to sing their old school songs, and the more frequently sung songs have become general favorites. A third type of party song is period songs. These help to reinforce the bonds of common memory between people of the same age group.

In considering the popularization of singing in Japan, we should not overlook the role of the amateur singing competitions broadcast on the radio by NHK, the national public network. The contests began in 1946, with the preliminaries held in local meeting halls and outdoor settings all over the country. This program provided a good opportunity for recreation and entertainment, especially in the postwar years when not much else was to be had.

Although karaoke is usually performed for fun, the spirit of these amateur singing contests lives on in yet another type of karaoke machine, one programmed to evaluate the singer. The machine not only allows you to sing, but assigns a score between one and one hundred. It is nearly impossible to achieve a perfect score, but someone occasionally manages to get a ninety-five. The fact that some bars offer a free bottle of whiskey to anyone who gets this score attests to just how few people do.

The machine's technique for evaluating a performer has little to do with the quality of the singing itself. It seems that points are given for such mechanical aspects as correctness of rhythm and strength of breathing. Even knowing this, taking on the machine remains a challenge.

This evaluation system is reminiscent of the one used in the NHK amateur singing competitions, which are now broadcast on TV. The NHK judges, themselves singing teachers, assign contestants to one of three categories: "not worthy of mention," "not too bad," and "winner." Rather than judging each performance on its own merits, they evaluate the singing according to a fixed frame of reference, awarding the "winning" status to those who meet this standard.

This approach to evaluation is quite common in Japan. The ranking systems of judo and kendo, for example, follow this pattern; the same principle also applies to disciplines such as flower arrangement, where students are awarded certificates at each level of achievement. The central role in most of these standardized evaluation systems is played by the iemoto or other qualified authorities of the discipline.

Nowadays popular songs are short-lived. It is said that the melodies sung by young people change about every three months. When a new song comes out, the karaoke version goes on sale almost simultaneously, and young people begin to practice it. Songs performed by professionals are no longer merely something to listen to and enjoy—they have become models to imitate.

The past several years have seen the rise in popularity of "karaoke boxes." These are small, soundproof rooms furnished with couches, tables, ashtrays, and a karaoke machine. They are most often used by friends, couples, or families. Some establishments serve light meals on request. Karaoke boxes may now be found all over Japan, especially in the parts of cities and towns devoted to leisure.

As an aid to self-expression and communication, karaoke can be enjoyed either individually or in a group. To make the fullest use of it, one should practice regularly. This concept has led to the invention of the Walkman-type karaoke machine—a light, portable unit with earphones.

Karaoke's function can be seen as an extension of two roles: that of the geisha who were valued for their entertainment and conversational skills at gatherings large and small, and that of the singing instructors (and on a simpler level, the song books), who helped keep the art of singing alive. In fact, we might call karaoke the mechanization of these roles. It has also become a social institution in its own right, the continual advances of the electronics industry adding new dimensions almost every year.

I have two predictions for karaoke. First, I think it may give rise to growing numbers of both amateur and professional singers, and at some point almost everyone will master the common language of song. Second, just as well-known hometown favorites are effective in breaking the ice at parties in Japan, one day people all over the world may communicate by means of "world favorites." Karaoke's potential for promoting international friendship has yet to be fully explored.

LIFESTYLE

Palanquins, Rickshaws, and Taxis:
A Tribute to Mini-Transport

Atsuko Tanaka

Japan is renowned for having some of the world's most efficient transportation services. These can be roughly divided into two categories—buses, trains, and other large vehicles designed to carry a lot of people at once; and taxis, which can accommodate only a few passengers. Ever since the development of the first horsecar line in Tokyo in the Meiji period, the government has backed mass transportation as a service essential to a modern nation. But the smaller vehicles—what we might call here "mini-transport" in comparison—boast a longer history and an appeal all their own.

The popular use of mini-transport dates back to the Edo period. In Japan, where horse-drawn carriages were unknown, the principal modes of land transportation in those days were horseback and palanquins. The common people were officially prohibited from using either of these, but in the town of Edo (present-day Tokyo) the custom of riding in palanquins, or *kago*, nevertheless became widespread among the masses.

The basic components of the kago were a passenger compartment made of woven bamboo, and a pole from which this structure hung. Palanquins had been used for certain purposes since ancient times, but during the Edo period they went through a process of diversification. Wealthy families and low-ranking lords rode in *hōsenji-kago*. Elderly and ill people and women were carried on *shite-kago*, literally "four-handed kago," so named because this simple structure was mounted on four bamboo poles. The *machi-kago* (town kago) that became popular in Kyoto and Osaka were used mostly in the vicinity of the pleasure quarters. Some versions invented later were *shinobi-kago* for lords and ladies,

71

rusu-kago for samurai and chief retainers, *tabi-kago* for travelers, and *shamo-kago* for transporting criminals.

Until about 1600 the common people went everywhere on foot, and palanquins were rarely seen in town. But within a quarter century, the kago was well on its way to becoming an integral part of the daily lives of people of every class. In a bid to counteract this trend, the feudal government prohibited the common people from riding in kago without a special reason, but unlicensed kago continued to proliferate.

Fearing that the common people would develop extravagant habits, the feudal government issued decree after decree to limit or prohibit the use of kago. In 1663 the number of commercial kago permitted to operate in Edo was officially fixed at six hundred—three hundred in town, one hundred at temples and shrines, and two hundred at administrative offices. In 1665 it was decreed that commoners could ride in kago on the highways leading out of Edo, but not within the city itself. In 1675, kago were once again permitted to operate in town to a limit of three hundred. Finally, in 1681, the general public was prohibited from using transportation devices altogether. Despite these efforts, however, kago increased rapidly along with the burgeoning popular culture of the early eighteenth century. Even women and children rode freely around the city in them. At one point, the number of kago reached 3,500. This popular transportation device had become an indispensable part of urban life.

In the early years of the Meiji era, the kago was eclipsed by a new form of mini-transport—the rickshaw, or *jinrikisha*, which appeared in 1871 and transported people on wheels for the first time. The use of this small carriage drawn by a man spread rapidly and had a much more immediate effect on city life than did the political change from Edo to Meiji. Within two or three years, this vehicle could be found in every corner of the country.

Novelty was not the only reason for the popularity of the jinrikisha. A ride in one cost only a fifth of the kago fare and was much faster—advantages that made it a highly convenient form of transportation not only for business purposes, but for mothers with small children and people on urgent errands.

To Western sensibilities, the idea of using a human rather than a horse to pull a vehicle may seem demeaning, but the Japanese did not think of it that way at all. When the feudal system gave way to the new world of Meiji, it was as if an era of liberation had dawned for the masses. These were people who had been accustomed to prostrating themselves whenever a lord's procession came along. They were always on the bottom looking up. No wonder they were elated by the feeling of comfort and grandeur they could now experience riding around in a jinrikisha, exploring the town at their leisure and literally looking down on other people. This feeling of freedom and superiority lent a great deal of impetus to the popularization of the jinrikisha.

Transport by palanquin. Above, men struggle to carry hefty sumo wrestlers; Edo period. Below, carriers pose with their foreign passengers on route over Hakone Mountain Pass, a particularly difficult trip; early Meiji period.

There were benefits for the men who pulled them, too. Becoming a jinrikisha puller required neither special skills nor a large cash outlay. In those days it was practically the only occupation a man could take up freely which drew a cash income and required only a strong, healthy body.

By 1873, two-thirds of the kago drivers had switched over to jinrikisha. The rapid popularization of this occupation gave rise to some abnormal situations, such as boys of twelve or thirteen working to support entire families, and seventy-year-old men pulling other, much younger men. These problems eventually resulted in the establishment of age restrictions for hauling jinrikisha.

In 1896, twenty-seven years after the jinrikisha first appeared, the number of these vehicles in Japan peaked at 210,688, including both the one- and two-passenger varieties. By this time the business of exporting was flourishing as well, to the point where manufacturers could barely keep up with demand. The number of jinrikisha exports was 4,623 in 1896, 10,097 in 1906, and 14,197 in 1910. The rickshaw went first to China, and soon spread through Southeast Asia. A few specimens found their way to England and Germany as curiosities, and later to America, Australia, and even Africa. The years before and after the turn of the twentieth century can truly be called the "golden age" of the jinrikisha.

When new modes of transportation came along, threatening to displace the jinrikisha—just as the latter had displaced the kago—pullers put up strong resistance. This conflict first made itself felt around 1872, when the Tokyo horsecar line opened between Shinbashi and Nihonbashi, and was to continue through the first years of the twentieth century. There had also been some resistance to the transition from kago to jinrikisha, but this was negligible compared to that which arose with the appearance of railways and trams. Indeed, whenever a railroad, horsecar line, or electric tramline was laid, there was trouble.

Motor vehicles first appeared in Japan in 1899. Needless to say, these were considered extremely luxurious commodities. In 1907 the nation's first trucking firm, called the Imperial Truck Transport Company, began to hire out two automobiles for passengers

Rickshaws on the
Ginza, 1874.

to offset deficits in their trucking operations. Similarly, the Japan Motor Vehicle Holding Company, established in 1909 to market foreign-made automobiles, took to hiring out its cars when sales were slow. These automobile-for-hire operations marked the beginning of Japan's taxi industry.

Taxis equipped with meters made their debut in 1917. Till then, automobiles-for-hire had operated on a time-based system; they now switched to a system based on distance, as indicated by the meter. The greater accuracy and economy of this method of fare calculation contributed to taxis' growth in popularity.

The period of prosperity in Japan that accompanied the outbreak of World War I provided a favorable environment for the steady growth of the taxi industry. In August 1912, a "taxi automobile company" opened near Sukiya bridge in Tokyo. That year the number of motor vehicles in the country, including trucks and passenger cars, totaled only 535. Taxi businesses were started next in Kyoto, Nagoya, and Osaka in 1914, 1915, and 1916 respectively, and the trend then spread to other cities nationwide. In 1916 there were 1,284 passenger cars in the country, and by 1921 the number had leaped to 8,265.

In 1925, the *en-taku* (one-yen taxis), which charged a fixed fare within a specific area, appeared in Osaka. Although the demand for transportation was leveling off at this time, small taxi companies continued to proliferate, resulting in a large gap between supply and demand. Frantic competition for passengers soon deteriorated into a price war that kept pushing fares lower and lower. By 1927 this situation had spread to Tokyo. The number of en-taku peaked in 1929–30, when taxis were operating at a fixed fare as low as fifty *sen*, or half a yen.

In the confusion during and after World War II, the pedicab, essentially a jinrikisha pulled by a bicycle, came into use as a substitute for taxis. Relics of this vehicle can still be found in the form of the *rintaku* seen in the city streets of Southeast Asia, and the rickshaws of India.

After the war, as Japan entered an age of peace, there was a resurgence of taxi activity. In 1946, the year the war ended, there were only 8,484 taxicabs in the whole country, but the number increased steadily, to 14,755 in 1950, 75,644 in 1960, and 253,917 in 1989.

It is interesting to note, however, that despite a steadily increasing demand, the number of taxicabs operating in large Japanese cities has not changed significantly in the last decade or so. This is because the authorities have suppressed any notable growth in order to prevent competition among the various taxi companies. Official policy holds that no company must ever be allowed to outstrip the others, and that none must fail. Customer convenience does not enter the picture at all.

✦   ✦   ✦

Taxis are safe and convenient. On the other hand, compared to mass transport, taking a taxi is rather expensive. Let us take a closer look at the continuing appeal of mini-transport.

A few years ago one taxi company began to provide a service it advertised with the slogan: "See the beautiful and historic sights of Kyoto by taxi!" Since then, the number of junior high and high school students using taxis on their school excursions has risen sharply year by year. The taxis take students on tours in groups of four or five per vehicle.

One reason for this trend among touring students is that the use of taxis allows them to plan their own itineraries; what's more, drivers not only take them where they want to go, but tell them about the histories of the shrines, temples, and other points of interest as they go. These detailed, conversational explanations go a lot further toward satisfying students' lively curiosity than do the canned speeches given on conventional bus tours. Another advantage is that students have a chance to experience personal contacts with the drivers as representatives of the local people. In short, although the time-based fares of large and medium-sized taxis are slightly more expensive than those of tour buses, taxi tours have become popular because they are more convenient and provide a living lesson in social studies.

+ + +

Structurally a taxi is a tightly closed space, and once you have entered it you are totally at the mercy of the driver. If you were to be spirited off somewhere, no one would notice. This is a potentially dangerous situation. Crimes associated with taxis, however, are extremely rare in Japan. Much more common are heart-warming stories of taxi drivers returning valuables and cash that their passengers have left behind. Women and elderly people do not even think about any threat of misdeeds by taxi drivers. At night, young women consider it safer to take a taxi than to walk.

Such cases are very rare, but one occasionally finds a taxi driver who takes advantage of a passenger's unfamiliarity with a neighborhood by taking a longer route than necessary. Cabs driven by this kind of rascal are called *kumosuke* taxis—"kumosuke" being the old term for kago drivers who did the same thing. But even taking this kind of exception into consideration, taxis in Japan are generally clean and safe, and their drivers honest.

Almost all Japanese taxis are equipped with automatic rear doors that save passengers the trouble of having to open and close them. This feature was invented around 1955. Some Japanese have had the embarrassing experience of flagging down a taxi in a foreign country, and standing on the curb waiting for the door to open.

The automatic door, however convenient, remains a non-human device. In Japan, where labor is very expensive, services performed by a human being are considered to have greater value than those done by a machine. In an attempt to provide higher quality service, one taxi company has its drivers jump out to open and close the doors for passengers manually. The drivers even engage in drills to speed up their performance. The customer is to be treated like royalty.

Some companies go even further. Their drivers are fitted out with uniforms created by well-known fashion designers, complete with hats and white gloves; these drivers perform their services with the same air adopted by employees of a high-class hotel. Passengers thus have a taste of the high life, if only for a short while. The cabs are always polished to a shine, the seats are clean, and the interior is fragrant with eau de cologne. One company in Kyoto even provides hot-towel service.

I would also mention here that when the taxi industry was first starting out in the 1910s and 1920s, taxi-driving was considered a prestigious occupation because these men, like airline pilots and ship captains, were entrusted with passengers' lives. In fact, many of the uniforms provided to drivers by the different companies seem designed to heighten and play up this association.

When people spend money on nonessentials like lottery tickets, pinball, or horse races, what they are actually doing is using part of their meager salaries to buy themselves a dream. Cities are places where dreams are for sale. In a similar vein, even people who are normally quite frugal treat themselves to an extravagant restaurant meal once in a while or splurge on some luxury product. The occasional ride in a taxi is a comparatively modest luxury that allows people to feel just a bit wealthy in the context of their everyday lives. Taxis are not only convenient and functional.

Taxis in front of Shinjuku Station, Tokyo.

The psychological attraction of mini-transport has not changed since the days of the kago and jinrikisha.

In conclusion, we might say the popularity of taxis in Japan is based primarily on the relative safety of the urban areas. Second, taxis provide a convenient, efficient way to get around quickly, and are sometimes useful to learn firsthand about an unfamiliar locality. Finally, taxis are cheap enough to be accessible on an occasional basis to most people, and luxurious enough to provide a momentary sense of grandeur.

Japanese Tableware: A Pottery Museum in Every Home

Masahiro Hikita

A typical table setting in most Western countries consists of round porcelain dishes of various sizes with a unified pattern. In most other countries, too, dishes are normally round or perhaps oblong, and items used at the same meal are likely to resemble each other in material and design. More often than not, little thought is given to the tableware used. At the Japanese table, however, dishes of diverse shapes, colors, and materials are combined with an eye toward aesthetic appeal, a practice that dates back to the Edo period, when it was an expression of the exuberant energy of the urban masses, who craved variety and novelty to enrich their daily lives.

The basic components of a Japanese meal are soup and rice. They are served in dissimilar vessels rather than matching ones: soup in a lacquered wooden bowl, rice in a porcelain one.

While lacquerware was used from ancient times, it did not come into general use until the the seventeenth century, when woodworkers from Ōmi were dispersed throughout the country. Previously, people had used fragile, unglazed ceramic bowls. Lacquer bowls gained in popularity and were used for both soup and rice until porcelain bowls were produced in large enough quantities to make them affordable. Even after these were adopted for rice, however, people continued to use lacquer bowls for soup, because they were lighter and kept liquids hot longer. During the past twenty-five years or so, however, cheap plastic imitations of lacquerware soup bowls have become popular for everyday household use.

By comparison, the use of porcelain in Japan is a recent development, dating back less than four hundred years. Porcelain

A Japanese meal with typical use of symmetrical and asymmetrical dishes.

production in Japan began around 1605, when Yi Cham Pyung, a Korean potter brought back by a warrior from Saga, discovered kaolin (the raw material for porcelain) at Izumiyama in Arita and used it to make white porcelain. The lord of Saga established a monopoly on the Arita technique in order to promote the industry in his realm, and began production, shipping from the nearby port of Imari, which eventually lent its name to the ware. From the

Meiji era, the misnomer was corrected and Imari ware became Arita ware (*Arita-yaki*).

After the introduction of Imari ware, the Seto region, which had been the nation's ceramic production center, sank into insignificance. In 1807, however, a Seto craftsman named Katō Tamikichi studied the porcelain-making technique in Arita, then returned to Seto to begin production there. Soon porcelain-making had spread throughout the country, and there was lively competition among the various regions. It was around this time that porcelain bowls began to appear on the tables of the common people in some localities.

Since it was only in the 1760s that the shogun is recorded to have first eaten rice from a porcelain bowl, it had thus taken a mere forty-odd years for this product, originally reserved for the elite, to make its way into the homes of ordinary townsfolk. The astonishing speed with which items of this kind came into popular use was a reflection of how urgently the masses were aspiring to a better lifestyle. It also indicates that the gap between those at the top and bottom of society was not as wide as we tend to suppose, even in the rigid caste society of the Edo period.

Toward the end of the nineteenth century, after porcelain rice bowls without lids began to be mass produced in Mino, they became inexpensive and popular. The establishment of a nationwide railway network, which facilitated long-distance transportation of heavy products at relatively low cost, contributed to their spread throughout the country.

Today's porcelain rice bowls are produced to high standards and fired at the considerably high temperature of 2350 degrees Fahrenheit (1300 degrees Centigrade). Because it is customary in Japan to lift soup and rice bowls from the table when eating from them, potters continually refined their technique to create lighter bowls. According to one authority, the old Imari rice bowls weighed 7 ounces (200 grams) on average, and those made in the middle to late nineteenth century, 6.3 ounces (180 grams). Decade by decade the weight continued to decrease, until today a rice bowl weighs only 3.5 ounces (100 grams).

Incidentally, the Japanese word for rice bowl is *chawan*, literally "tea bowl." This type of bowl was originally used as that—for drinking tea. The word "chawan" later became a generic term for ceramic tableware in general, and rice bowls in particular.

+ + +

Rice and soup bowls have remained round, but other types of dishes flaunt a rich variety of shapes. This trend first emerged in the midst of the popularization of ceramic ware during the Edo period, when peace and stability prevailed and merchants prospered. It was then that the bowls called *hachi* were invented to accommodate the fish and vegetable dishes these newly affluent people had started including in their meals to supplement their basic diet of soup and rice. Shallow porcelain *sa-hachi* and the deeper earthenware *donburi-bachi*, or simply *donburi*, were produced in various shapes and patterns with a number of different clays. Each new bowl was named after the food served in it.

Nor were plates necessarily round. In the Edo period, for example, there were the flower-shaped *kikyō-zara* ("bellflower plates"), as well as rectangular, square, and asymmetrical plates. They, too, were classified according to the kind of food served on them—raw fish, vinegared fish salad, boiled food, sweets, and so forth.

According to the potter Tōkurō Katō, the originator of the tableware culture was Furuta Oribe (1544–1615), a feudal lord and tea master:

> Oribe was truly a great designer. It was through his efforts that Japanese-style pottery came into being. Oribe was the person who set in motion the process of developing various glazes and designs. Most of these innovations concerned items for the tea ceremony. He would cut out colored paper in the shapes and motifs he wanted and paste them onto the orders he sent to the potters of Seto, Mino, Iga, Bizen, and Karatsu. These designs dominated the times and can still be found in textiles and ceramics today.
>
> Oribe created unprecedented shapes that might

be considered distorted or playful. Whatever the design or color, he had his own distinctive style. His predecessor, Rikyū, had had a more medieval bent of mind, looking toward death rather than the affirmation of life. For this reason, he was not particularly fond of variety in his tea bowls. Oribe, however, had epicurean tastes.

Oribe also placed special emphasis on tableware. In his day, people were in the process of supplementing the basic diet of rice and soup with new types of food. The new foods were served in or on small bowls or plates called *mukōzuke*. Oribe designed mukōzuke in numerous shapes and colors.

Mukōzuke dishes, which were not lifted during the meal, did not have to be light and easy to hold. On the other hand, in kaiseki-ryōri, the formal Japanese full-course dinner, the food was served on individual small tables or trays, and mukōzuke that did not fit onto them would be useless. Oribe's designs met both functional and aesthetic requirements. This is something he did exceptionally well.

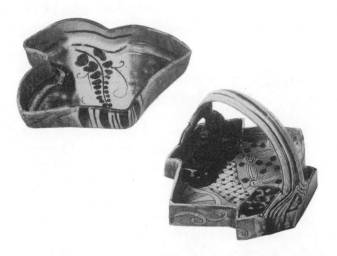

Oribe *mukōzuke* pieces.

Before Oribe's time, the only items placed on a meal table were a rice bowl, soup bowl, and perhaps a small plate. All were round and unremarkable. During Oribe's lifetime, however, people were starting to include side dishes, which they placed behind the soup and rice. Because the side dishes were not lifted during the meal, mukōzuke could have any shape at all, which allowed Oribe to give free reign to his imagination.

It has been pointed out that his aesthetic sense, which leaned toward distorted, abstract shapes, was of the same order as the aesthetic of *kabuki* (or *kabukimono*), a concept that enjoyed great popularity in the Edo period and even earlier. The word itself meant a tilt in something normally vertical, but it was used broadly to describe unconventional art forms, weird dress and hairstyles, and anything that deviated from its traditional or expected mode. Kabuki drama had its origin in this as well. All such forms had a comical or playful aspect to them; it was no coincidence that this sort of aesthetic thrived in the urban society of the Edo period. After years of war, peace had finally come. There was a chaotic energy among the masses, who delighted in momentary pleasures and freedom of expression. The new aesthetic was definitely not typical of the orderly society of the countryside.

Oribe's predecessor and teacher was Sen-no-Rikyū (1522–91), founder of the Senke line of tea masters that still dominates the tea-ceremony world today. Rikyū was forced to commit ritual suicide (*seppuku* or harakiri) by the warlord Toyotomi Hideyoshi, and when Oribe fell out of favor with Tokugawa Ieyasu twenty-three years later, he was ordered to do the same. But for a quarter of a century Oribe was Japan's foremost tea master, instructor to the shoguns, and artistic leader. Throughout his career he had many superb tea bowls and dishes made to order at the different pottery centers, setting in motion a trend that has continued to the present day.

The uniqueness of Japanese tableware culture was not lost on foreigners who came to Japan. J. F. van Overmeer Fisscher, a Dutchman who arrived in the early nineteenth century, recorded his admiration for the beauty and diversity of all the lacquerware and porcelain vessels he saw in the homes of people he visited. S. W. Williams, who accompanied Commodore Perry to Japan at the end of the Edo period, marveled at the wonderful, high-quality porcelain ware, and speculated that the Japanese could probably make pottery in any shape at all.

This was how tableware, which normally functions only as a vessel for serving food, became for the Japanese a means of diversion and a form of decorative art. The tendency to dress up their household articles is apparent even today. Not satisfied with objects that are merely functional, Japanese feel they must have beauty, too.

It is significant that this flair manifested itself in the realm of tableware as soon as the common people developed the means to rise above their bare subsistence diet. While the innovations themselves may have been introduced by gifted individuals like Oribe, they were embraced with amazing speed and enthusiasm by an urban populace eager for every indulgence in an era of peace and stability.

+ + +

Today, Japanese households have not only Japanese tableware, but Western and Chinese as well, making for quite a large collection. Having adopted culinary habits that include Japanese, Western, and Chinese food, each requiring a particular style of tableware, the Japanese are faced with the need to stock a wide variety of dishes and utensils.

This does not mean Japanese households have as many Western dishes as you would expect to find in a European home. In one survey, Europeans were found to stock about three times as many of each Western item as the Japanese did. The one exception, however, was coffee cups, which were about equal in number. This suggests that one of the first ways westernization made its way into Japanese daily life was in the realm of entertaining guests.

Japanese household articles in general have become westernized in recent times, and the value of chinaware imported from England and other parts of Europe has increased year by year. This in turn has prompted large Japanese tableware manufacturers to develop their own lines of dining sets. Often featuring traditional patterns such as cherry blossoms, these dishes are suited to both Western and Japanese cuisine, and represent a merging of Eastern and Western tableware, which until recent years had developed independently of each other.

This new ambiguity has led to some interesting combinations: with Western food now an integral part of the Japanese diet, it is likely to be served on a Western plate and eaten with a knife and fork; but if it is a side dish in a basically Japanese meal with rice, it will be eaten with chopsticks.

What we need now is tableware created specifically to suit the present-day Japanese lifestyle. As more women enter the work force, they have less time to spend in the kitchen. Women are also beginning to resent their role of cooking alone, and of getting up frequently during the meal to serve while everyone else relaxes at the table.

Two dining styles that partly overcome these problems are cooking at the table and serving food in one large dish from which

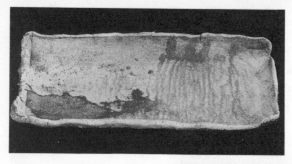

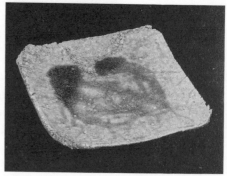

Large stoneware serving platters, fired in a traditional kiln, are still used in many homes and restaurants. Iga-Shigaraki ware with pools of natural ash glaze. By Shiro Tsujimura.

people can help themselves. A useful product here is the deep-dish hot plate, for grilling or simmering foods right at the table. Stews, sukiyaki, *shabu-shabu*, and other dishes that require only minimum advance preparation are easily handled with this new appliance, which four out of five Japanese families now use. Many households are finding uses for Lazy Susans and sets consisting of a large plate or bowl with matching small dishes, often in nontraditional artistic designs.

These are only a few of the innovations appearing one after another to meet the functional and aesthetic demands of the modern Japanese table. I wonder if any of them will have the resilience of the mukōzuke, which, after nearly four hundred years, can still be found in Japanese homes and traditional restaurants today.

Eating Out—At Home

Naomichi Ishige

If you look through the address book in a typical Japanese home you are sure to find in with the numbers of friends and relatives those of the neighborhood sushi and noodle shops. These are not there for the purpose of calling ahead to make dining reservations, but for ordering home delivery. The same holds true of the office Rolodex. When it is too much trouble to go out for lunch, working people often have lunch delivered right to their desks.

A highly developed meal delivery service has been one of the attractions of the Japanese dining industry since premodern times. In recent years traffic congestion and labor shortages have forced many shops to discontinue this service, but until about the 1960s almost all restaurants delivered meals without charge.

Meal delivery in Japan originated in the Edo period, when large numbers of restaurants began to operate in the major cities. These establishments catered mainly to ordinary townspeople rather than to the aristocratic and samurai/warrior classes. In Europe, similar developments were taking place at about the same time. The first restaurants appeared in Paris during the period before and after the revolution. Before that, fine cuisine had been reserved for the tables of the aristocracy, whose households employed professional cooks. With the collapse of the class system, the newly risen bourgeoisie established restaurants where anyone could come and enjoy a fine meal.

Under the Japanese feudal system, the samurai were in the upper strata of society just below the nobility, and the merchants in the lower ranks. The samurai, as the privileged class, continued to maintain their authority over society in an official sense until 1867, but in reality eighteenth-century Japanese society was manipulated not by the samurai but by the powerful merchants who controlled the nation's commercial wealth. By the middle of that century, Japan had become, in effect, a civilian society with the merchants at its core.

This period saw the rise of a number of new businesses, including restaurants catering to a bourgeois clientele. Once started, commercial restaurants spread rapidly, especially in the larger cities of Kyoto, Osaka, and Edo (present-day Tokyo). Because these cities did not fall under the control of a particular lord, there existed an atmosphere of freedom somewhat removed from the constraints of the feudal system. Their citizens tended toward the consumption-oriented philosophy of the commercial world rather than the frugality promoted by feudalism.

According to an 1804 survey, there were 6,165 restaurants operating in fixed premises in Edo at that time, or one for every 170 residents. The number of eating spots was actually greater than this, since not only were many restaurants uncounted but the survey excluded the numerous pushcart vendors operating in the streets of Edo. When all figures are taken into account, it is quite possible that nineteenth-century Edo had the greatest concentration of eating and drinking establishments of any city in the world. This proliferation of shops, and the competition it spawned, spurred the development of the meal delivery system.

+ + +

Japan has two types of meal delivery service: *shidashi* and *demae*. The word "shidashi" refers to delivery of a proper full-course meal, or parts of such a meal. It connotes high-class cuisine served to a well-to-do clientele. In the cities, however, even ordinary households make use of shidashi on such special occasions as funerals and memorial services.

Shidashi is provided by restaurants and cookshops. The latter prepare food for delivery only and have no dining facilities on the premises. Some cookshops will cater a meal, sending a cook to the customer's home to prepare food on the spot for a function or party.

It is in Kyoto, the religious and artistic center of Japan, that shops specializing in shidashi have flourished. Visitors from all over the country come to Kyoto to attend religious and cultural events, congregating at temples or participating in functions involving traditional arts such as flower arrangement, tea ceremony, and Noh and Kyōgen theater. In the midst of these cultural experiences, they expect traditional Kyoto cuisine rather than, say, Western or Chinese food.

This is where the long-established cookshops play an important role. Not only do they deliver meals for hundreds of people to the sites where functions are held, but they also service small numbers of guests at inns and teahouses. Some inns in Kyoto cook only breakfast on the premises and do not employ a professional cook. For dinner, they cater to guests' requests simply by calling a restaurant or shidashi shop for full-course meals. The meal might consist of as many as ten different dishes, the attention to detail and quality comparing favorably to that of a high-class restaurant. So carefully planned is the service that the food is sometimes delivered in two shifts to enable guests to savor the freshness of each dish. All the inn personnel have to do is serve the food, and perhaps warm up the soup.

Similarly, in teahouses, where customers sip saké while watching geisha perform, there is usually no cooking done on the premises. When a customer wants a meal, the proprietor simply picks up the telephone.

In times past, the main function of shidashi establishments was not to serve visitors from outside the city but to deliver cooked food to clients in their own neighborhoods. In the Edo period, Kyoto and Osaka were populated by large numbers of self-employed craftspeople and merchants, whose homes served also as workshops or stores. Not only was it frequently necessary to serve meals to business guests, but there were often assistants or apprentices who slept at their employer's house.

To supplement the plain meal prepared for their employees, many families ordered an extra dish or two for themselves from the shidashi shops. Even when the family ate a simple evening meal, it was common to serve an extra dish to the head of the household who, particularly until World War II, was a figure of great authority. Since preparing a special dish for only one or two people was not only bothersome but uneconomical, a good number of households adopted the custom of ordering one item a day on a regular basis from a cookshop.

So common was the practice in Kyoto that there was said to be one shidashi shop in every neighborhood. These shops were thoroughly versed in the needs of their clients' households: they knew the sexes and ages of family members, the preferences and favorite foods of each member, and the tableware in each kitchen. They became, in a sense, the neighborhood "database." It was not without reason that, in the course of arranging a marriage, inquiries into a family's reputation included a visit to the local shidashi shop. Some shops were even known to arrange matches among their clients.

The cuisine associated with shidashi is comparable in quality and variety to that of a good catering service in the West. By contrast, the service called "demae" provides light meals from the sorts of shops where ordinary people drop in for a casual lunch.

While shidashi shops prepare meals or dishes according to the individual client's preference and budget, demae customers order from the standard restaurant menu. Restaurants offering demae service often distribute their menus to households and offices in their neighborhoods to encourage phone-in orders.

Unlike shidashi, which provides all or part of a full-course meal, a demae order usually consists of a single, filling dish such as noodles, sushi, or *donburi-mono*, this last named after the large porcelain bowl, or donburi, the food comes in. Two of the most popular donburi-mono are *oyako donburi*, literally "parent-child donburi," consisting of rice topped with chicken and egg; and *unagi donburi*, rice topped with broiled eel. This "meal-in-a-dish" is in many ways analogous to the sandwich: not only does it make use of a favorite staple, but it is simple, light, and convenient.

Demae orders are normally paid for on delivery, but regular customers may be billed at the end of the month. The empty containers need not be washed—they are simply left outside the door to be collected later. Since disposable chopsticks are also provided, people ordering demae can enjoy their meal without once setting foot in the kitchen.

People are most apt to use demae when they are too busy to cook, when unexpected guests make a sudden appearance, or when a late-night meal is desired. Demae is also welcome as a nice change of pace from the usual family fare, particularly with such dishes as sushi that benefit from a professional touch.

Demae developed in the *shitamachi*, the downtown commercial and entertainment districts of the Edo-period cities. This was because the lords and their samurai retainers, who lived in the uptown *yamate* districts, did not generally patronize restaurants and demae services. Not only had these guardians of the feudal system been raised with an ideology hostile to commercialism, but samurai of high status looked down on the type of cooking associated with demae, considering it vulgar and dirty.

The downtown districts, on the other hand, were home to large numbers of merchants and artisans. Both good restaurants and cheap eating houses sprang up to serve them. The wealthier merchants patronized the former, while the artisans, whose overall income was not very great but who received some cash payments every day, were good customers of the latter. As activity expanded in Edo, the new political center, the city underwent rapid expansion. It also fell victim to frequent fires. A large population of carpenters and other tradespeople connected with the construction industry sprang up, creating yet another market for the eateries.

A downtown street in the nineteenth century was certain to have a noodle shop and a sushi shop, as well as other restaurants. It is said that in the livelier neighborhoods, over half the shops on the main streets were eating and drinking places.

✦ ✦ ✦

With the exception of sushi and the odd cold-noodle dish, demae meals are generally hot—and this creates the problem of how to deliver it before it cools off. In the Edo period, deliveries were made on foot by a shop employee carrying donburi bowls in a box. This was possible because every neighborhood had several shops within walking distance.

Modernization brought about a succession of changes in

Delivery by motorbike.

delivery methods. When bicycles became popular at the end of the nineteenth century, for example, they were immediately used for demae. If noodles in soup were placed on the carrier, though, there was the danger that the vibrations might cause the soup to spill. To get around this problem, delivery people soon became adept at balancing five or six bowls in one hand while steering the bike with the other, or even riding with the bowls balanced on their head.

In the 1950s, when Japan's motorcycle industry began to flourish, demae deliveries were made on small motorbikes fitted with carriers made especially for this purpose. Initially, the carrier was suspended from a pole by a spring to prevent the vibrations from causing spills. This eventually gave way to an enclosed rack with its own suspension system. Now, in addition to demae delivered by automobile, there are three-wheeled mini-motorbikes designed specifically for this purpose. You might see them scurrying about town, zipping between lanes of congested traffic.

In the earlier half of this century, when telephones were not yet widespread in Japan, phone orders for shidashi and demae came mostly from offices, stores, and wealthy households. The number of food shops that had telephones to accept such orders was limited as well. Since both the ordering and delivery of demae had to be done on foot or by bicycle, the service was available only to people who lived or worked in urban districts where eating places were plentiful.

This situation changed in the 1960s, when telephones made their way into practically every household. Now that it was possible to order demae simply by picking up the phone, and to deliver it hot within a fairly large radius by motorbike, residents of less-populated districts that might not be able to support shops on their own could finally enjoy this convenient service too.

+ + +

The modernization of Japan after the Meiji Restoration of 1867 was not limited to political and social transformations, but extended to every aspect of daily life, including food. The most revolutionary aspect of the "modernization of the stomach" was the introduction of meat into the diet. Needless to say, as food habits changed, new dishes became available to restaurant and demae clients.

Under the influence of Buddhism, the Japanese had lived on a meatless diet for about a thousand years. The taboo on meat evaporated in the modernization process, when the Meiji government promoted meat consumption to improve the physical stature of the people and introduced it into the army diet.

Because traditional Japanese cooking had not included meat, however, techniques for preparing it had to be learned from Western and Chinese cookery. Soon Western- and Chinese-style restaurants were springing up all over, and it was not long before they too were providing their own demae services. One of the most popular demae dishes today is *rāmen*—Chinese-style noodles in a savory soup stock of chicken or pork, or both.

While demae became available to rural households in the 1960s, that was also the time when food delivery services began to run into difficulties. Economic growth led to an increase in automobiles and traffic, making it difficult for delivery vehicles to maneuver through the congested city streets. But this was not all. The expanding industrial sector absorbed more and more of the work force, leading to a nationwide labor shortage, and restaurant proprietors could no longer be certain of having employees to spare for deliveries. Then, when long hours and wages became a major public issue, many shops could no longer afford to stay open late at night. As a result, it has become almost impossible to order in a midnight meal.

At present, only about 20 percent of the noodle shops in Japan still offer demae service. In the wake of these developments, one food that has stepped in to fill the gap and come to enjoy tremendous popularity is instant noodles. This product, which requires only the addition of hot water, comes in hundreds of varieties, most of them variations on the basic rāmen dish, a popular demae staple.

Japan now consumes over four billion packages of instant noodles a year. This amounts to more than forty packages per capita, from infants to grandmothers. Japan also exports these instant noodles to over eighty countries, producing it locally in more than ten. It is estimated that the number of units produced worldwide now exceeds eight billion annually.

Around the world people are sitting down to a bowl of instant noodles. Many of them might be surprised to learn that its origins go back to the lively downtown neighborhoods of the Edo period, where the Japanese first became accustomed to the convenience of demae.

Tapping the Riches of Night Soil

Takahiro Hisa

One inescapable fact of city life is that as the multitudes go about their daily business they generate massive quantities of waste. Whenever a new substance is discovered or invented, a new waste product appears. Our present age, for example, has witnessed the birth of nuclear waste, a product so dangerous it throws into question the very survival of the human race. Among the various waste materials, however, the one unchanging, ever-present substance that has plagued city-dwellers generation after generation and century after century is our own bodily waste. Since ancient times, people in urban areas have racked their brains for solutions to the ongoing dilemma of how to dispose of this product, created by the very state of being alive.

The estimated daily production of feces in a city of a million people is about 150 tons. In a city of ten million, like Tokyo, this figure rises to 1,500 tons. Add to this the daily volume of urine, one or two liters per person, and you will get some idea of the mind-boggling volume of human waste that cities must dispose of every twenty-four hours.

The need to worry about one's own bodily waste is a phenomenon peculiar to human beings, and to city dwellers in particular. Why are we the only creatures continuously harassed by this question? The reason is simple: our bodily wastes have become detached from the cycle that returns them to nature. Feces are meant to be transformed into soil with time. This is what happens to the droppings of wild creatures; and some farmers still put their own excrement into the fields as fertilizer. In modern cities, however, where there are few or no fields to fertilize, people's excrement has become a superfluous product requiring regular disposal.

A LOOK AT EUROPE'S PAST

The medieval cities of Europe had no sewers for waste disposal, and people living on upper floors simply emptied their chamber pots into the streets. The famous sewers of Paris, which provided the setting for the novel *Les Misérables*, date back to 1370, but their original purpose was to drain off rain. Human waste was directed into sewers for the first time in London in 1815, and in Paris in 1880. The number of people they served was limited, though, and most citizens continued to practice the same methods of waste disposal as before.

To rectify these unhygienic conditions, modern European city planners sought to make sewers universally available. All human waste was to be flushed into them with water. Banishing excrement from sight with one flush did clean things up as far as the immediate surroundings were concerned. It was a perfect example of the "philosophy of exclusion" fundamental to modern city planning. By removing everything dirty or aberrant, planners created cities that gave the outward appearance of being clean and safe.

There was one problem, though. Since there were no sewage treatment plants at that time, sewage simply flowed untreated into the rivers. As a result, the River Seine in Paris and the Thames River in London soon turned into foul-smelling waste disposal dumps.

The world's first sewage treatment facility was a settling tank constructed in London in 1889. Sewage treatment plants using the activated sludge process common today did not appear until 1928.

EASTERN AND WESTERN CONCEPTS OF HUMAN WASTE DISPOSAL

Modern times have seen remarkable progress in the treatment and disposal of human waste—but the philosophy behind the process has barely changed at all. Excrement is flushed speedily from sight, collected at treatment plants, processed, and thrown away. The West, at least, has held to an unbroken tradition of looking upon human excrement as a useless product best gotten rid of quickly.

One critic of this way of thinking, environmental engineer Sim Van der Ryn, points out the essential contradictions of present-day sewage systems in his book *The Toilet Papers*, published in 1978. As an alternative, he suggests a method of recycling human waste into compost by means of a device called a "compost toilet." He is also full of praise for the methods employed in premodern Japan—using excrement generated in the cities to fertilize the surrounding farms—which he considers an excellent example of a way in which human waste can be made a beneficial, reusable commodity.

Thanks to the practice of recycling urban human waste, premodern Japanese cities were noted to be considerably more hygienic than their counterparts elsewhere. For example, Edward S. Morse, an American who visited Japan in 1877, recorded the following impressions in his volume *Japan Day by Day*:

> Somewhat astonished at learning that the death-rate of Tokyo was lower than that of Boston, I made some inquiries about health matters. I found that those diseases which at home are attributed to bad drainage, imperfect water closets, and the like seem to be unknown or rare, and this freedom from such complaints is probably due to the fact that all excrementitious matter is carried out of the city by men who utilize it for their farms and rice-fields.

Susan B. Hanley, a professor of Japanese history at the University of Washington, analyzes the reasons for the high level of sanitation of Japanese cities of the Edo period in an essay published in 1989, "Urban Sanitation in Preindustrial Japan." Here she points out that although these cities, including Edo (present-day Tokyo) with its one million residents, were among the most heavily populated in the world, their per capita death rate was no higher than that of rural areas. She attributes this to their excellent water supply and waste disposal systems, and concludes:

> The Japanese have lived in a densely populated society for nearly a millennium and have learned to live with limited resources on the 15 percent of the land

that is not mountainous. By the Tokugawa period, the Japanese had evolved a lifestyle that enabled them to maintain large urban populations, and this may well be part of the key to the success Japan enjoys today. Clearly Edo seems to have been a more healthful city to live in than Paris or London were in the eighteenth and nineteenth centuries.

SEWAGE DISPOSAL IN PREMODERN JAPAN

There is nothing unique about the use of human waste as fertilizer. In fact, it is a common sight in rural villages, particularly in East Asia. In Japan the practice began about seven hundred years ago during the Kamakura period, when the technique was imported from China. The waste-recycling system of the Edo period was unusual, however, in that it took place not on a small cycle within a farming village, but as a large-scale operation linking city and countryside. Human waste, or night soil, was a commodity occupying a vital place in the economy; its recycling had developed into a regular industry.

The practice of using urban excrement as compost in the countryside became common in the mid-Edo period, that is, from the late seventeenth century through the early eighteenth century. This development was directly related to the growth of suburban agriculture. To provide the swelling numbers of city dwellers with fresh vegetables, farmers had to grow them just outside the urban areas, in large quantities.

With some of the world's most heavily populated cities as its markets, Japanese suburban agriculture flourished—supported by night soil gathered from those very cities. In other words, a remarkable cycle was set up in which human waste, a nuisance for and of no practical value to the city itself, was used as fertilizer in the farming villages, then returned to the city in the form of produce. Not only did a pattern of this kind arise between each city and its own suburban farms, but in an even larger cycle, the surplus night soil from Osaka was transported to Edo.

At the beginning of the Edo period, suburban farmers bartered vegetables for night soil, but this custom gradually gave way to

Roadside toilet. At right, two men react to the ambience.

cash sales. In Osaka the amount of feces produced by ten households over one year was said to be worth about 1.5 *ryo* in gold. Considering that a single ryo could keep one person in rice for one year, night soil was clearly a valuable commodity. According to Edward S. Morse's record made at the beginning of the Meiji era, if three persons occupied a room together in a flimsy tenement house in Hiroshima, their urine and feces paid for one person's rent

When night soil became this valuable, direct trading between farmers and urban dwellers became unfeasible. Farmers were frantic to secure their supply, while urban residents were determined to get the highest possible price. This resulted in frequent struggles over night soil and disputes about payment. There were even cases of theft of the commodity by struggling farmers.

Finally the suburban farmers formed unions to secure for themselves the right to buy excrement—but even then there was no end to their feuding among themselves. In 1772, the town magistrate of Osaka tried to regulate the situation by organizing 314 farming villages into "rural night soil collection corporations," allotting each the right to collect night soil from a particular urban district.

In the cities, too, things became more complicated. In Osaka, the right to sell feces belonged to the landlord, while the right to sell urine was the tenant's. Waste from samurai households fetched a higher price than that of ordinary townspeople. (Because samurai ate better food, they were thought to produce higher quality night soil.) In Edo, meanwhile, the right to collect night soil from the household of a lord was a rare honor. These rights were often monopolized by village heads and other wealthy farmers.

As human waste gained in value, dealers emerged who specialized in the product. These were the urine brokers and sewage transporters. In Edo, when the night soil business reached its peak, the total value of related transactions was said to be about 80,000 ryo a year. This was without a doubt a leading industry.

In eastern Edo, night soil was transported along the Sumida and Ara rivers, causing a certain amount of trouble for local residents. Some accounts note that when transport boats pulled into the docks, crowds of prostitutes came running out to meet them with shouts of welcome. The transporters brought back farm produce from the suburbs to sell on the open market, a practice that drew complaints from the regular vegetable vendors. Another object of contention was the stench the excrement gave off.

There were periodic movements to deny the transport boats entry to the ports; dealers warded these off by threatening to stop buying excrement altogether. Knowing full well that the cities would be thrown into confusion if the night soil business were discontinued, the authorities were obliged to let transport dealers have their way.

A NEW VERSION OF RECYCLING HUMAN WASTE

With the construction of public sewers and the appearance of chemical fertilizers, demand for night soil declined steadily. In recent years, however, a modern version of the old practice has emerged. This involves producing fertilizer by converting the sludge that remains after the process of sewage treatment.

The reasons for this development are many. First, the problem of how to treat the ever-increasing volume of sludge has become critical, and converting it into compost is one way to recycle it. Other recycling efforts have involved mixing the ashes from incinerated sludge into building materials and drying it for use as fuel.

A second reason for promoting the conversion of sludge into fertilizer is that people have started to have their doubts about artificial fertilizers. When chemical preparations first appeared on the market, farmers found them effective and convenient. Just as people might boost their energy with vitamin pills and other nutritional supplements, farmlands fertilized artificially show a remarkable, if temporary, increase in productivity. We now know, though, that the continuous use of chemicals causes soil to harden and lose its ability to absorb water.

Soil suited to raising crops has a crumbly structure, with spaces between the particles that facilitate ventilation, drainage, and moisture retention. Such a crumbly texture cannot be maintained without the presence of microbes that live in the soil. The microbes take organic matter into their bodies and decompose it, in the process secreting a viscous substance that binds the soil particles into crumbs. These microbes disappear from soil fertilized with chemicals. Artificial fertilizer may be easily absorbed by plants, but because it is inorganic it cannot provide nourishment for microbes.

Another problem is that if crops receive too much artificial fertilizer, they tend to grow progressively weaker. Plants accustomed to absorbing nutrients easily do not send their roots deep into the ground. Since roots close to the surface are easily influenced by fluctuations in temperature, such plants are vulnerable to the slightest change in the weather. Their resistance to disease weakens, making it necessary to treat them with other chemicals to kill off disease-causing microbes. In the process, any beneficial microbes present in the soil are eliminated as well, causing the quality of the soil to deteriorate still further. In addition, prolonged use of these chemicals is harmful to human farmers and consumers.

Replacing the natural cycle, then, with an artificial one sets off a chain reaction of related environmental problems. The only way to solve these is to restore the structure of the environment to its original form. Not only are agricultural chemicals a shortsighted means to increase yields, but they throw the whole system out of kilter. Modern thinking in general reflects this dangerous tendency to ignore the overall picture in favor of quick solutions.

Now that agriculture has clearly suffered from excessive use of artificial fertilizers and agricultural chemicals, greater numbers of farmers are returning to organic cultivation methods. The health boom has given further impetus to this trend by stimulating consumer demand for organic vegetables. Even people who are not particularly concerned with environmental issues have come to recognize the health benefits of eating chemical-free vegetables.

For various reasons, however, it remains difficult for some farmers to produce their own compost. With the advance of the single-crop system of growing vegetables, there is now no chaff or straw to use as a compost ingredient. Mechanization has eliminated the use of beasts of burden, which were formerly a good source of manure. It seems, too, that after decades of using artificial fertilizer, many farmers have lost their knowledge of how to make and use compost.

In response to this problem, businesses have sprung up around the country that specialize in processing sludge into fertilizer and distributing it as a packaged product. Like other recycling projects, they have not yet seen much of a profit, but some municipal entities do provide them with subsidies for their contributions to local urban sanitation.

THE FUTURE DEPENDS ON RECYCLING

The human race will never shake the need to dispose of its own waste. Although it would be ideal if each of us could use our own "product" for compost, this is obviously not a practicable solution for cities. What we need is a recycling system between city and countryside, similar to that of the Edo period—with the difference that the substance to be processed into compost would be not raw waste, but treated sewage sludge. The expression "between city and countryside" might be rephrased to read "between areas of consumption and areas of production." It is important to close the cycle as much as possible by returning all waste generated by consumption back to the production process. This principle applies not only to sewage, but to all consumer activities.

The sludge from city sewers should be returned to farms as compost. Since the number of farms in Japan is steadily decreasing, however, there may come a time when the demand for compost will be insufficient to absorb the huge amounts of sludge produced by the cities. Here we might look to the example of the eighteenth century, when extra night soil from Kyoto and Osaka was transported to the Edo suburbs. This was a large-scale system aimed at maintaining a balance between supply and demand.

Applying the same principle to present-day conditions, imagine a global system in which superfluous sludge from industrial nations could be converted into compost and recycled to agricultural producer nations. Like the sewage transport boats of the Edo period, the freight ships that export compost could bring back produce.

Are we going to keep squandering our resources and end up buried alive in our own waste—or are we ready to make recycling a reality? I believe that our ability to create restorative cycles in all our consumer activities will be the key to the survival not only of our cities, but of the human race.

The Story of Kimono

Kayoko Aikawa

The kimono developed in the mid-sixteenth century from two distinct prototypes. The first was the *kosode*, a robe of wadded silk worn beneath the wide-sleeved costume of nobles long before the Edo period. Attire had gradually gotten simpler, starting in about the fourteenth century, and at some point people began to wear the kosode as an outer garment. (The same phenomenon occurred in the West, where the undershirt was the forerunner of the T-shirt.) The second prototype was the *tsutsusode* (literally "tubular sleeves"), a similar garment with narrower sleeves worn by laborers and others whose work required greater freedom of movement.

In the process of becoming an item of outerwear during the latter part of the sixteenth century, the kosode, originally a plain white garment, began to appear in colored and patterned versions. Throughout the Edo period, various trends in color, pattern, and fit of both kimono and sash (*obi*) came and went until the kosode reached its present form—as today's kimono.

✢ ✢ ✢

The kimono, as well as many other elements of traditional Japanese lifestyle of the premodern age, evolved in the cities. The growth of commerce and industry from the fifteenth century resulted in the rise of a bourgeoisie class, which then became the driving force behind the development of various artistic disciplines, including traditional forms of song and dance, the tea ceremony, and flower arrangement. These disciplines created demand for specialized clothing and equipment, and the techniques for producing them made striking advances during the Edo period.

This period also saw a brisk flow of goods and information between the cities and outlying regions. Most of the textile production centers throughout Japan today, each with its own distinctive style, were established during the Edo period to serve the consumers of Edo (present-day Tokyo), Kyoto, and Osaka.

When it came to clothing and accessories, products made in Kyoto were considered superior. People in other parts of the country were delighted to receive *kudarimono* or high-quality textiles sent from Kyoto. Many trends in kosode patterns originated in Kyoto as well.

Kosode styles were often named after the eras in which they appeared; a few examples would be the *Keichō kosode, Kanbun kosode,* and *Genroku kosode.* A number of different dyeing techniques were developed as well, including *tsujigabana-zome* (patterns of diagonal stripes scattered with leaf-clusters), *chaya-zome* (landscape prints produced with indigo), *yūzen-zome* (landscapes in various colors), *kanoko-shibori* (a dappled effect), *komon* (a pat-

Young women wearing *Genroku kosode*. Kyoto.

tern of the repetition of small motifs), and *chūgata* (medium-sized prints). Each of these styles and dyeing techniques played a vital role in the styles of its time.

The mass publication of illustrated kosode books called *hinagatabon* began in the mid-seventeenth century and continued through the early nineteenth century. That as many as 180 books, each offering numerous examples of a single technique or style, were published during those years suggests that demand for kosode was not limited to the upper classes, but extended to the common people as well. The first hinagatabon were hand-drawn, but as the townsfolk became more prosperous and better able to afford luxuries, demand rose to such proportions that it became necessary to resort to using woodblocks to produce the images in larger quantities.

TRENDSETTERS OF THE EDO PERIOD

The fashion leaders of Europe in the seventeenth century were queens and noblewomen, whose personal styles were reflected in the dress and accessories of their times. By contrast, only one noblewoman in seventeenth-century Japan can be considered to have played any significant role in setting fashion trends. This was Tōfuku Mon'in, daughter of the shogun Tokugawa Hidetada and consort of Emperor Gomizuno-o. With powerful financial backing from the shogunate, this woman injected a new, more worldly spirit into the aristocratic court culture of the capital in Kyoto. A record of the costumes made for her, contained in a book preserved by the kimono-cloth shop Kariganeya, reveals patterns that accurately reflect fashions prevalent in the early seventeenth century. Generally called *Kanbun kosode*, this style of garment was worn by members of the ruling class and commoners alike.

Two other sources of fashion trends were the pleasure quarters and the world of Kabuki. Both of these underwent striking development as venues of recreation for the urban masses from the late seventeenth century on.

Within the restricted world of the licensed pleasure quarters, townspeople were able to escape the confines of the feudal system and express themselves freely. This freedom gave rise to popular styles, such as the long *haori* coat, that reflected the tastes of courtesans and teahouse girls.

Kabuki actors too, especially those who specialized in female roles, were leaders of trends in women's fashion. Some popular favorites that spring to mind here are *Ichimatsu-moyō* (a black-and-white checkered pattern), *Rokō-cha* (an auburn-tinged yellow dye), *Hanshirō-kanoko* (a dappled flax-leaf pattern), and *Kichiya-musubi* (a particular style of tying the obi)—all named after Kabuki stars. These are only a few examples from a lengthy list of popular patterns, colors, obi-tying methods, hairstyles, headpieces, and footwear that originated with the Kabuki theater.

During the Edo period, certain kinds of costumes came to be associated with specific annual celebrations and soon penetrated the life of the common people. Examples of these were the gala kimono ensemble worn at the New Year and the *yukata*, a simple, unlined cotton version of the kimono worn to religious festivals. There were also special outfits appropriate to viewing the different flowers that bloomed over the year. In this environment, the wives of affluent men began to vie with one another to see who would be seen in public in the most beautiful attire. These "contests," which functioned as the equivalent of today's fashion shows, added further impetus to the popularization of fashion-consciousness among the common people.

+ + +

Another group of people whose contributions were essential to the urban fashion scene were, of course, the artisans and merchants. From the early Edo period on, the cities of Edo, Kyoto, and Osaka have functioned not only as centers of consumption, but as production and distribution centers as well.

One enlightening account of urban artisans may be found in a book called *Jinrin kinmō-zui*, published in 1690. This mentions various kinds of artisans involved in the production of dyed and woven items—including needleworkers, engravers, bleachers, dyers who specialized in particular colors, chintz makers, brocade trimmers, weavers, dappled pattern makers, cotton beaters, and braid makers. The textiles and accessories these artisans produced were distributed to the public by the kimono-cloth shops that came into prominence in the late seventeenth century. One of the first such shops was Echigoya (now Mitsukoshi Department Store), established in 1673. Until then, fabrics had been marketed at industrial trade shows and private parlor sales to which only lords, retainers of the shogun, and prosperous merchants were invited. In other words, the possibility of buying these products had been limited to the privileged class. The clientele targeted by Echigoya, however, was none other than the urban masses. Some of the business innovations that contributed to the success of this venture were the acceptance of cash right in the shop, the setting of fixed prices (as opposed to negotiating with each client), and cutting fabric to specifications rather than selling it only by the bolt.

From the second half of the seventeenth century, urban consumer demand soared, and wealth began to accumulate in the hands of the tradespeople. The result was that these people themselves became an important consumer group. The new sales methods practiced by Echigoya were effective in meeting the demand of the trading class, whose influence was on the rise. Enterprises of this kind made a vital contribution to the popularization of fashion by bringing kimono cloth into the hands of the masses and, in the process, stimulating enormous demand. They also provided the practical support for the fashions generated in the pleasure quarters and the Kabuki world. In this sense, they were the prototypes for the department stores that promoted fashion initiatives beginning in the Meiji era.

In 1692 a publication appeared called *Shokoku kaimono chōhōki* (Shopping handbook for the various regions), consisting of profiles of various artisans, craftspeople, and merchants, as well as lists of fine items and specialty goods from around the country. The stated purpose of compiling this collection was to "facilitate purchases by providing the reader with information on what products are available and where to buy them." The early eighteenth century saw the debut of various manuals on how to carry out merchandise transactions; and another book, published in 1813, provided detailed, illustrated instructions on dressing for special occasions. The large cities of the Edo period, like today's huge urban centers, were information societies where news flowed abundantly on all topics, including fashion.

✛ ✛ ✛

Following the Meiji Restoration in 1867, Western-style clothing became the popular choice for any public situation related specifically to the country's modernization. The most striking instance of this change was the westernization of the ceremonial and working clothes worn by government officials. The introduction of this element of Western European civilization at the official level reflected the new government's determination to model itself on Europe and the United States in its efforts to modernize the country.

In the fashion world, however, the focus stayed on kimono. In other words, the government's sudden move toward "Europeanization" did not immediately spread to the public at large. The first thing that happened, rather, was that Western fabrics and accessories were incorporated into kimono outfits.

Women in Western dress tinkering with the latest Western import—a piano. 1880s.

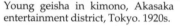

Young geisha in kimono, Akasaka
entertainment district, Tokyo. 1920s.

Teenage girl in her "Sunday best."
Meiji period.

In 1886, a kimono-cloth shop called Shirokiya began to sell the
azuma, a Japanese coat made of wool. Around this time, too, pur-
ple and brown cashmere were first used for the *hakama* (long
skirts) worn by schoolgirls; flannel and serge were welcomed
as materials for unlined spring or autumn garments; and mus-
lin printed with a colorful *yūzen* pattern became popular as a
new, westernized form that resembled traditional Japanese crepe.
Typical schoolgirl styles at the turn of the twentieth century included hakama worn with Western shoes, and foreign hairstyles
using wide ribbons.

Western accessories such as brooches, rings, parasols, and
handbags came to be used as accessories for kimono. The brooches
were pinned to kimono neckpieces or used as obi clasps. As the
use of precious stones slowly caught on, Japanese-made cuff links
and tiepins began to appear in shops.

Early in the twentieth century, some kimono-cloth shops that
had been in business since the Edo period expanded into department stores modeled on those of the West. At that point these

shops vastly increased the variety of goods they sold, while keeping their main focus on fabrics. Each department store established its own textile design section, which created new kimono patterns; these were very successful in influencing popular kimono fashion.

Some stores began to issue periodicals to keep shoppers informed of the latest fashion trends and storewide developments. Corresponding to today's fashion magazines, they were illustrated with photographs of the principal items offered for sale. The shops also started to offer mail-order service for customers living in outlying regions. The periodicals were discontinued before or during World War II, but some, including Mitsukoshi's, have been revived in recent years.

+ + +

During wartime, from 1930 to 1945, the kimono was rejected as everyday wear, in favor of more practical traditional forms. This was also a time when many people came to recognize the functional advantages of Western attire and to view the long sleeves, wide sash, and long wraparound robe of kimono as cumbersome. The clothing recommended for use in wartime consisted of the simplified kimono-type garments seen in the preceding eras of Meiji and Taisho, as well as outfits patterned on peasant work clothes.

After 1945, many people switched directly from wartime to Western clothing, which they considered more sensible and comfortable than kimono. The influx of American culture, stimulated by the presence of the Occupation forces and their families, resulted in the borrowing of every conceivable Western custom, from styles of housing to systems of city organization. This was a revolutionary chapter in Japanese cultural history.

The westernization of everyday dress was also reflected in educational trends. Needlework classes, which had always been an important component of girls' education, had previously focused on sewing kimono; after the war the emphasis switched to Western sewing. There was a rapid increase in Western sewing schools for women, from 400 with 45,000 students in 1947, to 2,700 with 500,000 students in 1955. At the same time, the focus of the fashion world shifted from kimono to Western clothing.

As the number of working women increased steadily, the kimono fell out of favor as everyday wear. Starting in about 1960, Western clothing became the mode of everyday dress for almost the entire urban population, with the exception of some elderly people and those whose jobs required traditional dress. For the most part, kimono came to be worn only on festive occasions.

The 1960s brought a mild backlash against the rapid Westernization of culture, as some critics pointed out a need to reevaluate the Western-Japanese "double life." It was in this decade that the kimono became a source of pride as the "folk costume" of Japan. Nonetheless, most people stopped sewing kimono and other traditional clothing at home, leaving their production to professional manufacturers.

Although the kimono had first developed in response to the needs of urban daily life, the westernization of cities and of Japanese life in general gradually resulted in a situation where it came to be considered unsuitable for everyday wear. The garment has not disappeared entirely from the Japanese lifestyle, however. Even today, kimono fabrics and accessories are produced in weaving centers around the nation, and glimpses of kimono-clad men, women, or children are not infrequent.

What are the occasions that still call for kimono?

One is marriage. During the ceremony itself, the bride and groom may wear either Japanese or Western wedding costumes, depending on whether they hold the rite at a shrine or church. The bride is also likely to appear in a colorful kimono at some point during the reception that follows. Most brides include several kimono ensembles in their trousseaus, as evidenced by the considerable number and variety of kimonos displayed in the bridal sections of department stores.

For most people, the kimono has become a festive or ceremonial garment worn only at certain annual events and rites of passage. In addition to marriage, these occasions include the first shrine visit of the New Year, the coming-of-age ceremony, funerals, and memorial services.

The kimono is also worn in connection with traditional

performing arts and as a working uniform in certain jobs. For example, it is worn by employees of Japanese-style inns and restaurants, as well as by geisha and their young apprentices, *maiko*.

I believe that the reason the kimono is still worn on formal occasions is that most such events continue to be conducted in a traditional manner. In other words, this form of dress is considered appropriate because the situations are traditional. Also contributing to the kimono's staying power may be that deeply embedded in the consciousness of many women there is admiration for beautiful kimonos, and a longing to wear them.

Now that kimonos are worn so infrequently, many parents neglect to teach their children how to put one on properly. As a result, the teaching of this art has become a profession. There are now schools all over the country that train young women in the techniques of putting on kimono and tying obi. Women may also be dressed in kimono by beauticians in beauty parlors.

The dichotomy between everyday life and special occasions remains an important aspect of Japanese culture. The use of the kimono once encompassed both festive and everyday dress, but now that daily life has become westernized, the kimono has taken on specialized significance as the costume for festive and ceremonial events. It is interesting to note that the last decade or so has seen a movement among some artists and intellectuals to reject this dichotomy and use the kimono as just another option for everyday wear.

In the lives of the modern generation, moreover, there are an increasing number of situations that cannot simply be categorized as either "everyday" or "special," but fall somewhere in between. The increasing complexity of modern life has created a demand for greater pluralism in many aspects of culture, including clothing. In addition to ceremonial and everyday dress, we now have party and evening wear, visiting wear, town wear, and other styles to suit various moods and occasions. The diversity of these new fashions reflects the multifaceted character of Japan's modern lifestyle.

The Japanese Home:
A Grab Bag of Tradition, Trends,
and High-Tech

Shōji Yoshino

In the large cities of Japan, locating a house by its address sometimes proves a nearly impossible task. Not only are street names
and house numbers often unposted or nonexistent, but residential
streets are laid out as haphazardly as a beginner's patchwork
quilt. As if that were not enough, a jumble of architectural types
increases the sense of disorder. It is not uncommon to see a
postmodern apartment building standing next to a traditional
tile-roofed wooden house, for example. This situation tends to
provoke sharp criticism among non-Japanese, who complain that
city planning in Japan is totally uncoordinated. On the other hand,
some foreigners find this aspect of Japanese cities exciting and
dynamic.

One reason for the haphazard development of the Japanese
urban landscape is that houses are generally made of wood and
are not built to last more than a few decades. Unlike towns
consisting of stone or brick buildings, a town of simple wooden
houses tends to change constantly. In the absence of strictly enforced long-term guidelines, different people build or rebuild at
different times and are unlikely to take the overall picture into
consideration.

In this discussion of the Japanese home, I would like to focus
on an aspect that has not received much attention despite its importance: the prefabricated nature of Japanese homes. Academic
definitions aside, I use the term "prefabricated," or "prefab," to
indicate a structure that can be assembled quickly and with relative ease from often modular parts.

Strictly speaking, the expression "prefab housing" (*purehabu
jūtaku*) is currently used in Japan to describe a relatively new type

116

of house assembled from mass-produced parts transported from the factories by truck to the desired location. Today, prefabricated homes account for about two hundred thousand houses a year in Japan, or 15 to 20 percent of the housing market. If we use my broader definition of "prefab," however, practically all Japanese wooden houses fall into this category, and have done so for centuries. Here I shall use the term "traditional prefab" to refer to the conventional building style, as opposed to the newer mass-production method.

Traditional prefab construction was already being practiced in the Edo period. Records left by early foreign visitors to Japan contain accounts of how the Japanese cut house parts out of wood, assembled them with remarkable skill, then later took them apart piece by piece and transported them to a different location for reassembling. The reports confirm the existence of the prefab concept in Japan long before it was introduced in the West early this century.

The prefab character of Japanese urban housing grew out of a building formula that uses wood, which is light and portable, to construct the framework of the house. The prefab mode was ideal for meeting the demands of premodern times, when frequent fires and the constant influx of people into the cities created an extremely large demand for cheap rental housing.

Although it may not be evident today, the history of Japanese residential construction consisted of two entirely different streams: the building of private residences, and the building of rental housing. In the former, the emphasis was on quality. The reason for this was not necessarily a desire to live in a house of high quality, but rather a fear that a mediocre residence would bring shame on the family. Particularly in the affluent sectors of society, the quality of one's residence was an important indicator of status. Cutting corners on labor and materials could result in a poorly constructed house that could be a source of embarrassment for generations to come. The artisans, who were under the patronage of the family for whom the house was being built, were well aware of this fear. They knew that if they did their job well, they would be rewarded by generation after generation of grateful clients. Artisans took great pride in receiving these special orders. Needless to say, not everyone had the means to patronize the better carpenters and craftsmen, and the practice was confined mostly to big merchants and wealthy landlords.

Rental housing was a different matter. The principal requirements for this type of construction were speed and economy. Consequently, the production and installation techniques were thoroughly systemized, and components were of the minimum permissible size. For tatami mats, ceilings, and the various sliding panels used as doors, windows, and room dividers, the builders used ready-made products in standard sizes. Some houses did not have tatami or fittings at all, the tenants being expected to provide their own. This arrangement was called *hadaka-kashi,* or "bare rental."

Another important distinction between the two types of housing was that each private residence was a one-of-a-kind order, while for the rental house the same models were reproduced over and over. There were, to be sure, some so-called high-class rental houses that resembled private residences, but they were the exceptions.

Many builders of rental homes were newcomers who came from various parts of the country to look for work. Because it was contract work rather than an ongoing relationship of patronage, there was frantic competition for jobs in this sector.

It is true that compared to Western methods, even private residential construction in those days might have appeared to be of the prefab type, but the contrast with rental-house building was striking, especially when it came to the attitudes of the artisans. As for the people who lived in the two types of housing, they belonged to two entirely different worlds.

In the past, when Tokyo was called Edo, there was a saying: "Fires are the flowers of Edo." Ostensibly an homage to the city's splendid firefighters, it also reflects the high frequency of damaging fires in the cities of those times. Every time there was a fire, large numbers of residents lost their homes and found themselves wandering the streets.

In the process of experiencing fire after fire, the people worked out strategies for dealing with these emergencies. Wealthy home-

Workers paint the walls of an upper-class residence with plasterlike sealant.

owners built fire-resistant storehouses where they kept food supplies, tools, furniture, and other household effects, taking out only everyday necessities as they needed them. They also built fire walls between buildings to contain damage.

People in rented lodgings had no such recourses. When a fire broke out, all they could do was pile their household belongings on a cart and flee. Their possessions may not have been worth much, but as long as they could take these items with them they did not suffer any direct loss.

Tenants living in a "bare rental" situation would escape in a cart with their stove, tatami mats, and house fittings. Because sizes were standardized, these people would be able to use everything in their next lodging. You might say the word "prefab" applied to their very lifestyle itself, because they could put it together, take it apart, and carry it wherever they wished.

When able to evacuate successfully, the tenants stood around cheering the firefighters on, like spectators in a stadium watching a soccer game. Wrote one foreigner in his diary, "It was exactly like a festival!"

As far as the tenants were concerned, perhaps it *was* a festival.

The only people who were more than superficially inconvenienced by the fires were, after all, the superintendents and landlords—whose high-handed, coercive manner of collecting the rent did not endear them to the general public. Moreover, a good number of the tenants were construction laborers, who stood to benefit from fires since they led to a sudden increase in the demand for construction, and more work.

For those who had left their hometowns to come to the cities and live in rented quarters, town life was an impermanent "floating world" (*ukiyo*). Because of the frequent fires, their homes were no more than provisional shelters, or makeshift "rabbit hutches," and the city was a place to drop anchor temporarily. Thus, unlike homeowners, they were not particularly concerned with the appearance or environment of their housing.

Another reason for this attitude was that tenants were excluded from local affairs. Only homeowners were recognized as official residents. Tenants paid no taxes, perhaps a blessing of sorts, but as a result they had no rights and no chance to participate in the community. While they may have dreamed of building their own house with a garden someday, or of having a shop on a main street, these were fantasies far beyond their reach.

Prefabricated rental houses were not specimens of good architecture, nor were they very comfortable, but they were conducive to an easygoing, carefree lifestyle. The tenants lived from day to day without worrying about the future, doing their best to enjoy themselves. Rather than spend their leisure time at home, they would leave their shabby dwellings for the lively sections of town, to enjoy a stroll about the amusement quarters or main streets. Occasionally, they might even be able to afford a visit to a house of pleasure. And since tenants accounted for 80 to 90 percent of the population of large cities, it was their lifestyle and inclinations that generated the customs, fashions, and pastimes of the popular culture we know today.

+ + +

Today, housing construction in Japan is going through an unprecedented transformation. This becomes obvious as soon as

"Instant" prefab home with more traditional-style units to right and rear.

Prefab homes in middle-class neighborhood.

you step out into the suburbs, where you will find a lively assortment of houses dressed up in fashions to suit every taste and fancy. Among them, of course, are mass-produced and traditional prefab houses, but there are also many "eclectic prefab" models—homes that combine traditional and modern modular elements. For example, a house might utilize a traditional wooden framework but employ mass-produced parts and materials for everything else, including the outside trimmings, roof, windows, inside trimmings, and floor. Or, conversely, a house might have a framework of the mass-produced type, but with trimmings, roof, and so forth designed in the traditional manner.

Eclectic prefabs emerged gradually at first, but then with increasing frequency after 1980. Since then, the development of the eclectic prefab has surged forward, with a proliferation of mass-produced parts and materials, and intense sales competition.

I have in front of me a set of three catalogues, each volume the size of a telephone directory, listing items offered by a particular company. They include interior trimming materials, sound-proofing materials, fittings for windows and doors, storage systems, storage units, kitchen fixtures, bathroom fixtures, exterior trimming materials, roofing materials, construction materials, lighting fixtures, lighting equipment, electrical materials, electrical fixtures, and much more.

There are 150,000 items in the catalogues, but because these products seem to reproduce like amoebas, the company employees say no one knows exactly how many items are currently available. And this is only a drop in the bucket, for there is also an astounding number of similar small-to-medium production firms.

Besides the combination of building techniques, what are some of the characteristics that distinguish eclectic prefab from other residential housing types?

First, there has been a growing tendency to ostentatious exteriors: white walls with decorative sidings, Victorian-style front doorways, roofs with dormers, and a medley of porches, fences, doors, and windows. This trend reflects a rejection of traditional Japanese values, which favored unobtrusive exteriors.

In a more practical vein, contractors are incorporating new storage features, such as under-the-floor bins and attic storerooms. Traditional Japanese houses are notoriously deficient in this respect. Indeed, one of the most troublesome problems besetting Japanese housewives has been how to deal with a lack of storage space, so innovations in this area have been well received. It is unfortunate that the architects themselves have shown so little enthusiasm about trying to improve storage capacity in the houses they design.

Parts and materials that simplify installation have gained rapid popularity among builders. Plastic is used for all kinds of items such as eaves, troughs, sidings, and roofing materials; veneer is in common use for interiors; and prefab bathroom and kitchen systems are now standard. Such developments have brought about sweeping changes in the content and scope of the carpenter's work, but these have been accepted with practically no resistance. Perhaps the approach itself is not all that new—in fact, there is something about it that brings to mind the rental house of the past.

Houses with both Japanese-style tatami rooms and Western-style wooden-floored rooms have become common now. In flooring there is a trend toward veneer, while fashions in interior finishings are in constant flux. Several years ago the wall covering of choice for Western-style rooms was veneer; this gave way to a white or off-white synthetic wallpaper called *kurosu* ("cloth") resembling either cloth or a textured paint job. There is not the slightest trace of traditional aesthetics here, but a whitish interior is thought to be bright and healthy. It seems that pragmatism is asserting itself ever more strongly.

The eclectic prefab phenomenon lets people realize their ideal lifestyle with a seemingly infinite selection of items, and seems suited to the modern Japanese consumer society. In fact, some house-planners now use computers to help customers plan their dream homes. As a result, the residential construction that has emerged in recent years is neither Japanese nor Western in style. If anything, it has shifted toward individual expression, a self-tailored style that might be expressed by the following formula:

$$[(\text{Japanese-style} + \text{Western-style} + \text{current fashion}) \times \text{high-tech}] \div 3$$

The contents of each element in the formula are filled in by contractor and customer. As the trend toward individual architectural style continues in both residential and commercial construction, there is no indication that coordinated urban landscapes are on the horizon for Japan, at least in the foreseeable future.

III

POLITICS AND ECONOMICS

How Bureaucrats Manage Society

Atsushi Ueda

There's a very old Japanese saying: "You have no chance against the authorities or a crying child." The "authorities" here referred to the officially appointed *jitō* (stewards) who administered the estates of medieval times. While the medieval stewards are no longer around, the Japanese people still feel that they have no choice but to submit to the dictates of their public officials.

Japan is generally believed to have become a democratic nation after World War II. I do not agree. I believe that although society has become democratic in many respects, Japan remains under bureaucratic rule. This means that for the past eight centuries, since the establishment of the steward system in the Kamakura period, officials have ruled the common people. In theory, it should be practically impossible for any authority to survive over several centuries. One axiom of human history is that when power structures continue for a long time, they eventually become corrupt and are overthrown by the people.

Does this mean, then, that Japanese officialdom is not a power structure? What else could it be? This is a question I first began thinking about when I became a public official myself—and even now that I have left the public service, the question continues to haunt me.

I grew up in Osaka and continental China. After graduating from university I went to Tokyo for the first time, to work in the headquarters of a certain government ministry. I was in for some big surprises.

I had imagined that a government office would be a feudalistic place where superiors ordered their underlings around. Imagine my shock when, on my first day at work, I saw a young staff member perched casually atop the section chief's desk, in lively conversation with him.

It also took me by surprise when several of my coworkers, ranging from ordinary staff to chief clerks, came to me, the newcomer, to confide their grievances with their superiors. They were also full of complaints about the work they were asked to do. It seemed that the place was smoldering with discontent.

I was extremely impressed by this. It struck me that a government office was a revolutionary place. Never before had I come across such people: mostly Tokyo University graduates, ultra-elite—but also revolutionary.

In the ten years I worked in that ministry I had many interesting experiences, but I shall mention only one, which happens to be most relevant to the discussion at hand. Around that time the Osaka-based Daimaru Department Store chain had just begun to expand its business to Tokyo, and the new branch at the Yaesu exit of Tokyo Station was the talk of the town. Before I knew it, my fellow workers had nicknamed me "Daimaru"—because I too came from Osaka.

As the only Osakan in the office at the time, I was treated as something of a curiosity. I suspect I was also subjected to a certain amount of special indoctrination. For example, various superiors made a point of mentioning to me that "public officials' *raison d'être* is to protect innocent citizens from wicked merchants." Gradually I came to realize that in their world view, the worst of the "wicked merchants" were the affluent businesspeople of the Osaka-Kyoto area. One particularly remarkable element of this indoctrination was the motto, "Don't be concerned about poverty, but about inequality." When you think about it, this is clearly a socialistic idea.

Democratic thought is said to have originated in the ancient Greek city-state of Athens. The English word "democracy" derives from the Greek *democratia*, a combination of *demos* (the people) and *cratia* (power, authority, rule). In other words, there is a clear distinction between democracy and other systems, such as monarchic or aristocratic rule, where the masses are governed by one person or a small group. "Rule by the people" means rule by the many.

This is a fine idea, but how does one bring it off? In ancient Greece, the unit of democracy was the *polis* (city state), and these were held down to a size that permitted all citizens to participate directly in decisions. When the population expands too much, such a system ceases to work.

England was the first country to institute general elections, and its parliamentary democracy soon became a model for the rest of the world. This is what we mean today by democracy. In brief, it is based on two principles: one, the adoption of policies by majority decision according to a system of representation, and two, the full implementation of these policies.

Japan, too, has a representative system and a national assembly known as the Diet. In this respect, it may seem at first glance that the government is democratic. A closer look at the legislative process, however, reveals that laws are proposed, debated, and decided upon not in the Diet, but in councils set up by the various ministries. These councils are organized almost entirely by bureaucrats. The laws and policies selected by the councils become government drafts, which are then presented to the various committees of the legislature.

At the end of this process, the drafts reach the floor of the Diet, which functions as little more than a place to ratify the bills. We might even go so far as to say that a Diet session is a kind of ceremonial performance, to give people inside and outside Japan the impression that decisions are being made democratically.

The reality, then, is that practically all the laws and policies of the Japanese nation are established by bureaucrats. What are we to make of this?

Strictly speaking, this is not democracy. We would do better to call it "rule by bureaucracy."

The next issue to consider is that of the full implementation of these laws and policies. In fact, the bureaucracy is in charge of implementation as well. Here we meet up with the concept of *gyōsei shidō* (administrative guidance)—which affords public officials a great deal of leeway in terms of using their own discretion to "make allowance" for circumstance. This authority is not recognized in the constitution, but it is a day-to-day reality.

A good illustration of the way administrative guidance works may be seen in the handling of speeding and parking violations. The regulations here are so strict it would be unrealistic to try to enforce them in full; the extent to which they are enforced is left entirely to the discretion of the officials concerned. Armed with these laws and regulations, they are free to clamp down on some people and be lenient with others, as they see fit. We are talking here about an incredible amount of power.

There is one redeeming factor, though. It is relatively rare for Japanese non-elected officials to be swayed by personal connections or bribery. In fact, we might say that herein lies the strong point of the Japanese bureaucratic system. So, on what basis *do* public servants make their case-by-case judgments?

I believe the answer to this question may be found in the ethic, "Don't be concerned about poverty, but inequality." Japanese officials do not believe that society can be managed by inflexible regulations alone. Instead, they use the extraordinary measure of administrative guidance to practice a kind of socialism that combats inequality. In a nutshell, poor people and struggling businesses can expect more lenient treatment than affluent people or successful businesses. Japan is a constitutional state, but the law is not everything; the role of administrative guidance gives the Japanese bureaucracy its distinctive character.

The scope and power of administrative guidance is well-known among individuals and corporations alike, yet no one tries to do away with it. Even in times of social and political upheaval, such as the Meiji Restoration or the end of World War II, it was business as usual for the bureaucracy. This is because people cannot imagine what would become of their society under any other system. They know Japan is ruled by bureaucrats, and are basically content with the arrangement.

When people in Western countries think of a national bureaucracy, they envision a group of officials who faithfully execute the law. In America, England, or France, for example, a public servant is almost a machine. In such countries, it would be unthinkable for public servants themselves to wield greater political power than any other group. But this is precisely the situation that exists in

Minamoto no Yoritomo, twelfth-century shogun who established an early feudalistic regulatory system influential to Japan's modern bureaucracy.

Japan, thanks to administrative guidance, the "heirloom sword" in the hands of the bureaucrats.

✛ ✛ ✛

The Japanese bureaucratic system as we know it today dates back to the network of guardians and stewards created by Minamoto no Yoritomo (1147–99), the first shogun of the Kamakura *bakufu*, or military government. These officials were members of a landed warrior class who had functioned as a kind of military police and served as temporary officers in times of war. When Yoritomo came to power in the late twelfth century, he organized them into a bureaucracy supporting the bakufu, and they came to be called samurai. The lord-retainer relationships established between the two groups reflected the feudalistic nature of the system. One significant point to keep in mind about Japan's bureaucratic structure, then, is that it arose in conjunction with feudalism at the dawn of the medieval period.

There were a number of subsequent developments in the system of guardians and stewards, but the greatest changes occurred in the wake of Oda Nobunaga's widespread construction of castle towns and Hideyoshi's geographical separation of samurai from peasants in the times immediately preceding the Edo period. These two warlords had triumphed over the various regional powers, including rival warlords and large religious establishments, and succeeded in consolidating the country under national rule. In the new order the samurai, who had been removed from their estates to the towns, lost their landholdings and their feudal ties with the peasantry but gained the right to manage national affairs. In other words, the old bureaucracy of feudal landlords was transformed into a bureaucracy of national administrators.

The drastic measures of Nobunaga and his successors led to the birth of 350 new cities, which sprang up around the 260 castle towns established throughout the country. These "mass cities" soon became gathering points for the huge numbers of people roaming about the country. At the nucleus of each was an administrative body of newly urbanized bureaucrats.

The removal of samurai from their land marked the beginning of a system that was to assign specific feudal functions to specific officials. In the older-style bureaucracy of the Kamakura and Muromachi periods, feudal lands had been assigned to lords, and each lord had been given responsibility for all the administrative functions in his own territory. The lords had clung to their pieces of land, staking everything on them, since they were the primary sources of their livelihood.

Why, then, when Toyotomi Hideyoshi announced his policy of cutting the feudal ties between samurai and peasants, did the members of this landed bureaucracy willingly acquiesce, and simply give up their land without a fight?

One important reason was that by this time the available means of accumulating wealth had expanded to include the mining and manufacturing industries and commerce. Since all these enterprises were closely interconnected, the strategy that surfaced as the surest road to economic success was an administrative system that promoted them as a whole. This was the background to the remarkable evolution of the Japanese bureaucracy as it shifted away from one kind of feudal system and reemerged in a different form.

+ + +

Tokugawa Ieyasu, founder of the Tokugawa shogunate, summed up the bureaucracy's philosophy with the words, "Allow no peasant to become extremely prosperous, nor any to be ruined." This meant that officials were to use their authority both to prevent failures and to suppress outstanding success. Salvation of the poor went hand-in-hand with clamping down on the rich.

It would be impossible to calculate the number of wealthy merchants who had their businesses confiscated for one reason or another during the Edo period. Finding fault with merchants and putting them out of business was no problem for the officials with their prerogative of administrative guidance. They exercised this prerogative freely, believing that too great a gap between the rich and poor would have had a disruptive influence on society. They also feared that wealthy individuals might gain enough power to threaten the authority of the officials, or even of the shogunate itself.

In every age, the catchphrases of the Japanese bureaucracy have been "equality," "welfare," "a simple lifestyle," and "regulation." The words the bureaucracy most dislikes are "disparity," "competition," "luxury," and "freedom." In other words, they have always had a very clear-cut sense of purpose.

Another reason for the system's extreme longevity is the very way it is organized. Although the bureaucracy itself has enormous power vis-à-vis society as a whole, this power is minutely divided up within the bureaucracy. The system distributes power among many, helping to keep the nation from lapsing into monarchic or aristocratic rule.

Power is divided along both regional and functional lines. Nowadays the regional divisions comprise the local public bodies of prefectures, cities, towns, and villages. The functional divisions are even more numerous, and include the various spheres where authorities issue the permits and licenses associated with every aspect of people's lives. These responsibilities are distributed among the ministries with their many bureaus, departments, and sections. Thus are the vertical and horizontal threads woven together to form a tight network of authority.

If we compare the Japanese administrative system with the traditional categories of monarchic rule, aristocratic rule, or democracy, we must conclude that it falls into none of these. It does bear some resemblance to aristocratic rule in that it *is* an oligarchy, placing power in the hands of a select group of people; yet there is no privileged ruling class in Japan corresponding to a hereditary aristocracy. In its present-day form, at least, the Japanese public service is open to citizens from all backgrounds, and posts cannot be passed down from parent to child.

For lack of a better word to describe the Japanese bureaucratic system, I would suggest calling it "feudalistic." Feudalism can be loosely defined as a many-layered power structure of territories or spheres of influence. The medieval feudal system involved the distribution of feudal estates and designation of lords. The modern bureaucratic system involves the distribution of functions and designation of authorities. In other words, the original territories consisting of domains of land have been replaced by functional territories. What remains unchanged is that responsibility is widely delegated, from the center out into the territories.

+ + +

The extent of the power held by bureaucrats places the general public in a somewhat absurd situation. We do not normally take much notice of it, but practically every single aspect of our lives is always being regulated by some government office.

Take, for example, the houses we live in. The houses themselves fall under the jurisdiction of the Construction Ministry, which issues detailed regulations governing form and structure. Most of the furnishings and household articles are manufactured according to the guidelines of the Ministry of International Trade and Industry (MITI), as is our clothing. Food is regulated by the Ministry of Agriculture, Forestry, and Fisheries; medications by the Health and Welfare Ministry; and art objects by the Cultural Affairs Agency. The water supply, sewage, electricity and gas, and telephone are controlled by Health and Welfare, Construction, MITI, and Postal Services respectively. If we step out into the garden, the trees and flowers we see are approved by Agriculture,

Forestry, and Fisheries, whereas any rocks in the garden are the responsibility of Construction.

The car, again, is MITI's. Of our pets or domestic animals, dogs and cats are the charge of Health and Welfare; cows, horses, and carp are controlled by Agriculture, Forestry, and Fisheries; and monkeys, goldfish, and tropical fish by Education. As for birds, pigeons are the responsibility of Postal Services; sparrows are that of Agriculture, Forestry, and Fisheries; and parrots that of Education.

The situation gets even more complicated when we consider human beings. At birth and for a time afterward, we are in the care of maternity hospitals and public health offices, which are the responsibility of the Health and Welfare Ministry. Educational facilities from kindergartens to universities are controlled by the Education Ministry; should we get arrested in the course of our student activism this involves the National Police Agency. When we graduate and get a job, we will fall under the jurisdiction of different authorities, depending on the kind of work we do. Whatever our job, though, one ministry that will never let us out of its sight is the Finance Ministry, home of the National Tax Agency. When we reach old age, we will rely once more on the care of the Health and Welfare Ministry—till we finally end up in a cemetery overseen by the Construction Ministry.

The multifarious branches of Japan's bureaucracy reach into every nook and cranny of our lives through their authority to grant permits and licenses, either to us directly, or to the people who provide us with products and services. Thanks to this system of thoroughgoing regulation, our lives and our country's industries are protected with regard to safety, hygiene, convenience, and economy. In return we pay our taxes and put up with endless rules and approval requirements. These rules, wielded by public officials, are not so different from the staff and whistle used by a shepherd for herding sheep.

As long as we obey the shepherd's commands we are safe and can expect to enjoy a reasonably comfortable standard of living. Just what is this "reasonably comfortable standard"? It actually refers to that of the officials themselves, for the lifestyle of public servants is meant to serve as a model for that of the public at large. The officials hope to draw people with lower living standards up to their own, but if anyone rises *above* this level, the officials begin to cast a cold eye their way.

It is a wonderful thing to have our standard of living assured in this way. Of course, it does not leave much room for freedom....

+ + +

In all fairness I would point out one more strong point of the feudalistic bureaucracy. This system of organizing and dividing up authority is conducive to intense competition among the officials themselves. The various ministries, and the departments and sections within them, constantly try to outdo one another in terms of achievements in their respective spheres. This gives the system a great deal of vitality.

As was mentioned earlier, positions in the Japanese bureaucracy are not hereditary, and capable people are recruited widely from the populace at large. If this were not the case, true competition would be impossible.

One aspect of this competitive atmosphere is that ideas are often generated from the bottom up, rather than from the top down. The people in high positions are forever scooping up new suggestions from their subordinates. In the central government bureaus, it is the assistant section heads who actually hold the administrative power. Even when section heads, department heads, and vice-ministers have decided on a course of action, nothing can proceed without the agreement of the assistant section head class. Each Japanese ministry and public agency has tens of thousands of these up-and-coming young bureaucrats.

The Japanese bureaucracy has evolved as a flexible, information-oriented body; rapid shifts in policy are common as officials gauge the changing trends of the times. If this were not so, how could we explain the incredible story of the Meiji Restoration, in which Edo capitulated without the shedding of blood, and dominion over peasants and land was transferred smoothly from the feudal lords to the emperor? American and European scholars of Japanese history are still struggling with this mystery.

Finally, a word about the financial basis of the Japanese bureaucracy. As in other countries, revenue comes from taxation—but it is important to note that most taxes are paid through corporations. Not only corporate taxes, but also individual income tax and even residential taxes are deducted at the source of income. Thus all tax revenue from salaried workers in the private sector comes to the national government and local public bodies through corporate accounts. You might say that, from the officials' point of view, the corporations constitute a kind of taxpaying association. This is precisely why officials are so intent on nurturing them. Promotion of industry is an eternal theme of Japan's bureaucracy.

At first glance, the essentially socialist philosophy of this bureaucracy and its ongoing cooperation with capitalist interests may seem a bit contradictory. Never, though, is competition among corporations allowed to heat up to the point of an all-out struggle for supremacy. Survival of the fittest is not on the agenda. "Allow no corporation to become extremely prosperous, nor any to be ruined," runs the revised slogan of the modern bureaucracy.

✦ ✦ ✦

The Japanese bureaucracy is indeed an ingeniously devised system; yet it does have its weak points. One is international diplomacy. Though Japanese officials know everything there is to know about domestic matters, they are hopelessly out of touch when it comes to other countries. A feudalistic bureaucracy is probably fated to fall into this trap, since the various power groups are so caught up in their round-the-clock competition with one another that they have neither the time nor the inclination to inform themselves on foreign affairs. They are interested in information from abroad only if it seems to have some bearing on the domestic scene. In other words, there is no foreign diplomacy in Japan: all diplomatic issues are handled as matters of domestic administration. This has caused countless foreign policy blunders, including those that got Japan into World War II.

Another problem is that the administrative ethic, "Don't be concerned about poverty, but inequality," is gradually losing its relevance in today's affluent society. I think the Japanese bureaucracy will soon need to take a fresh look at its overall program.

For instance, one of the most pitiful aspects of life in this supposedly affluent society stems from official land policy. It is common knowledge that impossibly high urban land prices are causing widespread feelings of helpless frustration among the populace. The bureaucracy ought to be devoting itself wholeheartedly to solving this problem.

Another important issue now confronting Japan and many other countries is the question of how to deal with an aging population. Will the competitive bureaucrats be able to marshal their wits to meet this challenge?

I believe the future of the Japanese bureaucratic system, for all its intelligence and long-standing tradition, will depend on its ability to respond flexibly to the new situations and problems facing the human race.

Japanese Taxes:
"Ours Is Not To Reason Why...."

Katsuhisa Moriya

In 1989 a general consumption tax was introduced in Japan for the first time. The 3 percent tax on all goods and services was meant to increase the annual tax revenue by trillions of yen, giving a much-needed boost to the government coffers. Nationwide opposition to the tax caused considerable political turbulence at the time, even leading to resignations of prime ministers and an Upper House election upset for the ruling party. Since then the furor has gradually died down, and the tax has now become a fact of life. There is even talk of raising it.

Because taxes are one of the top concerns of citizens everywhere, taxation issues are always a major factor affecting the course of politics. Let us look at the kinds of taxation that exist in Japan.

First, Japanese taxes can be divided roughly into three categories: direct, indirect, and regional. There are four types of direct tax, eighteen types of indirect tax, and twenty-eight types of regional tax. Direct and indirect taxes are paid into the national treasury, while regional taxes go to local governments. There are two broad categories of regional tax: regular taxes and taxes levied for specific purposes. Within the regional category, a clear differentiation is made between prefectural taxes and city, town, or village taxes.

From the description so far, the uninitiated might get the impression that taxation in Japan is fairly straightforward and easy to understand. Nothing could be farther from the truth. Not only are there a great many kinds of taxes, but the competition to develop new ones causes the situation to change with such dizzying speed that even the experts find it difficult to keep up.

While there is no official count of how many types of taxes there are in Japan, the total number would undoubtedly run into the hundreds.

The number of different taxes is not the only problem. Rates, too, differ widely, and may range from 1 or 2 percent to more than 50 percent. One does not have to be a professional to realize that the collection of income tax or customs duties could be done much more cheaply and efficiently if each type of tax were levied on the basis of a uniform percentage. Instead, the rates vary according to all kinds of complicated elements—graduated taxation and taxation by weight, for example—not to mention the tax policies and theories of the moment, which add to the overall complexity. As a result, Japan's taxation system has become far removed from the people, who find it increasingly difficult to understand.

Although there is a great deal of discussion about taxes, the bottom line is that citizens everywhere wish to pay as little tax as possible, or better still, none at all. The attitude of the government, of course, is just the contrary. From the standpoint of the national finances, the more taxes people pay, the better. The emotionally charged struggle between these two fundamentally opposed positions goes back to ancient times when the "nation" was first invented as a mode of organization.

The problem with a "nation" is that once it gets started, there is no end to the amount of money it consumes. Nor would it do to stop it in midstream. If the nation were to run out of money it would immediately collapse; and with all control lost, the population would revert to its former uncivilized condition. In ancient times there were countless examples of this very phenomenon.

Even though there are many problems associated with running a nation, few people would deny that it is still the most effective device of civilization available to us at this time. Such being the case, we have no choice but to give financial support to our nation through taxes, whether we like it or not.

+   +   +

While the custom of offering tribute to monarchs goes back to the birth of the monarchic system itself, taxation as such did not begin in Japan until the establishment of a legal system after the Taika Reform in the seventh century. The first taxation system was part of the program to strengthen the power of the state under the emperor.

The system consisted of four basic components. The first was the rice paddy tax, levied on all rice paddies. The unit of taxation was a sheaf of rice, and the rate was 3 percent. The second component was a tax paid in labor, the third a tax on produce other than grain, such as textiles, fish, or lumber, and the fourth was another labor tax. A fifth component, in the form of a miscellaneous tax, was added later.

This orderly tax system functioned well as long as the populace and farmlands were administered conscientiously; but as imperial power grew steadily weaker, the system began to disintegrate. The "aristocratization" of the politicians and bureaucrats stimulated the growth of the manorial system with its private domains, giving rise to various lucrative privileges. The state was powerless to interfere with this process. Under these circumstances, a consistent national taxation system was bound to break down. The dissolution spread rapidly from the middle of the Heian period.

This does not mean that the national taxation system under the imperial authority disappeared altogether. Rather, it was reduced to a mere shell, and pushed to the sidelines by the complicated mess of taxation practices associated with medieval feudalism.

The tax systems that developed under the manorial system are too numerous to mention, but the taxes themselves fell basically into two categories: those paid in kind, and those paid in labor, corresponding to the components of the national taxation system described earlier. Matters did not stop here, however. The very nature of the feudal lords' authority gave rise to ever-increasing complications in the tax-collection situation. In later medieval times, the various types of manorial and tax-collecting authorities had become so intertwined within each domain that the "tax system" was well on its way to becoming something more like a "kickback system." As if this were not enough, the *bakufu*, as the national public administrative authority, instituted a string of arbitrary miscellaneous taxes one after another, with no attempt whatsoever to create a consistent or systematic taxation policy.

It is easy to dismiss this chaotic state of affairs as a typical medieval phenomenon, but for the people on the paying end, taxation had become a complicated and inscrutable nightmare. It was not even profitable for those on the receiving end. For most absentee lords residing in the large city of Kyoto, the high cost of tax collection made it difficult to secure a sufficient annual revenue. Furthermore, as the regional warlords grew more powerful, lords living in cities found themselves losing their manors, while at the same time the power of the court nobles and religious institutions of Kyoto began to decline.

Anti-tax movements are nothing new

The disarray of the medieval tax system was simply another proof that the state was not doing much of what a state ought to be doing. Certain people were determined to change all this. These were the warlords struggling to establish a unified power structure.

Two warlords who came close to realizing this goal were Oda Nobunaga and Toyotomi Hideyoshi. The latter did in fact succeed in setting up a unified national government. Part of his program for revolutionizing the medieval state was to execute a fundamental reform of the taxation system. It involved a thorough land survey that clarified once and for all who the true landowners were, and who should be paying the taxes.

Because Hideyoshi's taxation system recognized only the two sharply distinguished categories of landowner and taxpayer, it met with strong opposition from powerful local warrior families who had been benefiting from kickbacks in the confusion of the former situation. Hideyoshi responded with all-out military force, not stopping until every vestige of opposition had been eradicated.

His reforms resulted in a taxation system that was consistent and easily understood. Because it eliminated the many intermediary layers of the kickback structure, however, it also contributed to the weakening of local warrior families by depriving them of their financial base. In other words, it created conditions that led naturally to the separation of warriors from peasants. By revolutioniz-

Farmers paying their taxes in rice. Official at top right monitors activity. Edo period.

ing the tax system, then, he also brought about a revolution of the social system and principles of state organization.

By promoting these revolutionary tax reforms, Hideyoshi's unified administration was able to effectively increase its tax revenue and establish a solid economic base. It was with this revenue that he implemented his grandiose plan to construct castle towns all over the country. It would not be an exaggeration to say that most of Japan's cities trace their origin back to Hideyoshi's tax reforms.

The principles of his taxation system were inherited by his successor, Tokugawa Ieyasu. One of the system's notable features was the preferential treatment given to large cities. Under the Tokugawa administration, Kyoto, Osaka, and Edo (present-day Tokyo) were exempted from paying land taxes. These three cities, which were under the direct rule of the shogunate, were the most important marketing and information centers in Japan. Without them, it would have been impossible to exercise state authority and maintain control over the nation.

As time went on, however, the Tokugawa government gradually modified this policy of preferential treatment. Although the exemption from land tax was maintained from beginning to end, the shogunate began to intensify the taxation of the urban merchants from around the end of the seventeenth century. For example, taxes on saké had already been in effect in the regional domains, but in 1697 the shogunate instituted a business tax on urban saké dealers for the first time. As saké production amounted to about one hundred and eighty million liters a year, and the rate of taxation was 50 percent of the selling price, this tax brought in a revenue of several hundred thousand *ryo*. From that time till the end of the Edo period, the shogunate continued to introduce a succession of new taxes on one business after another. As Kyoto, Osaka, Edo, and other cities flourished, the expansion of their economic activities stimulated changes in government taxation policies, which had originally been geared to a more rural economy.

To procure its initial capital, the new government of the Meiji Restoration which began in 1867 instituted sweeping land-tax reforms. Although the government went through the motions of setting up a modern nation, the industrial structure was dominated by agriculture, and the leaders could not envision any large-scale source of tax revenue other than land. For the new government, therefore, the base for taxation was the land tax.

The land-tax reforms, which involved determining land classifications and values for taxation purposes, were implemented in every region without exception. When you consider that the French were not able to achieve such a large-scale tax reform even after a bloody revolution, this was quite amazing. Needless to say, the Meiji reformers encountered strong resistance, with anti–tax reform riots erupting all over the country. This could be considered the most revolutionary reform program in Japan since the Taika Reform of the seventh century.

Through political compromise the Meiji administration succeeded in carrying out its tax reforms. In so doing, it was able to avoid national bankruptcy; but the revenue from the land tax was not sufficient to foster the growth of modern industry, nor to support the nation in its quest for greater prosperity and military strength. In other words, it could not provide the massive capital required to create a modern state.

The Meiji politicians and bureaucrats were aware of this. After studying taxation systems in Europe and America, they set out to increase their tax revenues by introducing direct taxation, based on the principle of individual income tax. The Income Tax Law was instituted in 1887, even before the establishment of the national constitution. (It is interesting to note that America did not have an income tax law until 1913, a quarter of a century later than Japan.) The Japanese income tax law was revised in 1899, at which time income was divided into three categories: corporate income, income from interests, and individual income.

In its quest for new sources of tax income, the government devised various tax policies one after another, but from the beginning to the end of the Meiji era, the tax system centered on such direct taxes as the land tax. It was not until the Taishō era in the 1910s and 1920s that the government introduced taxes collected in a less visible manner—called "indirect tax." With this, the tax money does not come out of the pocket of the person who actually pays it to the government. It includes all taxes on services and commodities, including luxury taxes, liquor tax, restaurant and hotel taxes, and other consumption taxes. At first the ratio of direct to indirect tax income was 30/70, but the ratio increased to 53/47 at the end of the 1920s, and to 60/40 in the Pacific War years.

After the war, the government promoted the Shoup Tax System, based on the recommendations of American economist Dr. C. S. Shoup. His particular interpretation of democracy involved equalization of the tax burden, as well as the idea that the responsibility for paying taxes is connected to the right to participate in democratic politics. These principles gave rise to a tax system centered on income tax and to the comprehensive graduated tax equation.

It is not clear whether these tax reforms spawned the period of high economic growth, but there is no doubt that the rampant consumer spending of the 1980s, especially in the cities, tempted the government to cash in on this trend by instituting a consumption tax. The idea arose from a perverted understanding of the advantages of indirect tax—namely, that the tax burden would be invisible and imposed equally on everyone. In reality, far from being invisible, the consumption tax is glaringly conspicuous, and affects the poor much more than the rich.

Will this consumption tax turn out to be another historically significant development, like Hideyoshi's tax system reforms and the land-tax reforms of the Meiji Restoration? It is still too soon to tell.

From Ancient Coins to the "High Yen": The Story of Japanese Money

Yōtarō Sakudō

The usual Japanese word for "money" is *o-kane*, a combination of the honorific prefix *o* and the word for gold or metal, *kane*. Another word, *o-ashi* or simply *ashi*, is a colloquial expression for "money" that has been in use since ancient times. The literal meaning of this second word is "foot." To understand how the Japanese came to refer to money as "foot," let us take a brief look at the history of Japanese currency.

Metallic currency appeared in Japan at an early date compared to other countries. The first coins were issued by the ancient government at Nara in 708, using copper sent to the Yamato court as a present from Chichibu District in the Musashi domain (Saitama Prefecture). Various coins began to circulate among the people in the subsequent Nara and Heian periods, but at the end of the tenth century minting operations were discontinued because of the government's weakening political influence and a shortage of copper ore. As a result, Japanese coins virtually disappeared from circulation, and the Japanese used currency imported from China instead.

The Japanese coins of the Nara and Heian periods were used as wages for official construction work, and for trading in the markets near the capital. Although the circulation of this currency was partial and local, it did represent the beginning of the use of money by the common people.

By the thirteenth century trade between Japan and China was flourishing, and there was a considerable flow of Chinese coins into Japan. The introduction of Chinese currency stimulated private counterfeiting operations within Japan, further increasing the amount of money in circulation. Compared to the Chinese coins, though, the copies produced in Japan were of poor quality.

By the sixteenth century, currency from China was being called by all kinds of names, one of which was the word meaning foot, o-ashi. The word reflected the differentiation of good-quality Chinese coins from copies. The former were welcomed on the circulation market everywhere—they "moved" around freely, like feet. The saying *Kane wa tenka no mawarimono* ("money goes around and around") indicates how conspicuous the function and mobility of money had become by this time.

We have seen that coins were used in transactions among commoners as early as the eighth century, and that money had become functional enough to be called o-ashi by the fifteenth century. It was not until the latter half of the seventeenth century, however, that currency in Japan became "mass currency," in the sense of circulating widely in towns and villages nationwide.

In 1636 the Tokugawa government began to issue its own coins to be used as the official currency of the regime. In the ensuing decades it continued to mint these coins in large quantities, eventually eliminating Chinese coins and standardizing the circulation of currency throughout the land. From the end of the seventeenth century on, it strongly promoted increases in currency volume to keep up with the development of the commercial economy.

During the 1660s and 1670s a new class of landed farmers emerged. At this time, there were striking developments in commercially-oriented agriculture, accompanied by the development

Officials examining and packing newly forged oblong coins. Edo period.

of rural processing industries. All these factors contributed to the firm establishment of the money economy.

It was during this era that the ruling clans of the feudal domains began issuing their own paper money, called *hansatsu* (*han* = feudal domain, *satsu* = paper currency). As a rule, this currency was valid only within the particular feudal domain where it was issued. Hansatsu were used in 244 domains, accounting for approximately 80 percent of the so-called three hundred lords.

The precursor of hansatsu was a form of private paper currency called *shisatsu*, used in various regions from the beginning of the Edo period. The shisatsu evolved from an earlier paper currency called *hagaki* which first appeared in Ise in what is now Mie Prefecture. Hagaki are thought to have developed from the notes used by the Ise merchants in their business transactions from the late Muromachi period, but there is no proof of this. The oldest hagaki in existence today is presumed to have been issued in 1610. In the context of world history, this is a very early date for paper currency. Predating even the "goldsmith notes" issued by the goldsmiths of London in 1640, the early appearance of the hagaki in Japan testifies to the advanced state of the money economy at the time. Also, the fact that both coins and paper appear to have originated in western Japan is an indication that economic development was more advanced there than in eastern Japan.

With the development of a commercial economy, money made it possible for commoners to transcend their station in life and become "cultured." The writer Ihara Saikaku (1642–93), in his book *Nippon Eitaigura* published in 1688, provides a clear account of this process, tracing it from the age of a few privileged merchants through the rise of a powerful new merchant class that included names such as Mitsui and Sumitomo, known today as corporate giants. This work portrays the growth of an economically-based society where money took the place of family lineage in determining the social status of the merchants.

One important area of commerce in which people amassed large fortunes during the Edo period was the money exchange business. The moneychangers, who had their own trade organizations or guilds from the early years of the Edo period on, functioned within the framework of a professional association that restrained competition, similar to the guilds of Europe. Supported by the shogunate government, the guilds had a spirit of solidarity, as well as religious and conservative overtones. Their activities were geared to protecting their own interests in order to strengthen their control over the market.

To maintain communal order, the guilds formed clubs or associations called *kō*. These were of two basic types: those with a religious character and those with an economic character. At first the religious implications were more pronounced, with members engaging mainly in the support and restoration of temples and shrines, and religious pilgrimages. Later, however, there were more groups with predominantly economic aims such as mutual assistance and relief financing. Mutual financing and loan associations that arranged financial benefits for their members also began to spring up, some on a national scale, and continued to develop as financial organizations for the general public in both cities and rural areas.

At the same time as the guild merchants were trying to preserve collective order and promote development by organizing kō, a number of powerful family enterprises were establishing groups called *kumi* by consolidating their capital to meet the fierce competition within each line of business. These groups, with names like "Mitsui-gumi" and "Kōnoike-gumi," were centered on a main family and supported by collaborating organizations built up by the branch families.

The framework of commercial capital in the Edo period was constructed out of these kō and kumi, which evolved systems of management to deal with the growth of the market economy. Later, they were to provide the base for the development of the *kaisha* (company or corporation) style of organization imported from European countries.

+ + +

The transition from Edo to Meiji was accompanied by radical changes in government policies concerning currency and finance.

The Story of Japanese Money 151

In May 1868, the authorities took measures to rectify the inconsistent monetary system by which eastern Japan used gold and western Japan used silver. From September of the same year, studies were begun on establishing a new Mint Bureau to replace the gold, silver, and copper mints of the Edo period. The Mint Bureau was set up in Osaka and began operations in 1871. The same year marked the enactment of the New Currency Law and the birth of the new unit of Japanese currency called "yen."

In connection with the establishment of the yen as the official currency of the nation, the government had to deal with the issue of the hansatsu, the paper currencies issued and circulated by 244 feudal clans. By the end of the Edo period these had developed into mass currencies used widely within the various domains in both urban and rural areas. Although in principle the use of hansatsu was supposed to be limited to the domain of issue, a great many exceptions to this rule occurred as the circulation of commodities transcended feudal boundaries. When a particular type of hansatsu became inconvertible, the crowds that converged on the hansatsu exchange houses to redeem their notes were a mixture of people from inside and outside the domain. This situation worsened to the point where hansatsu riots were expanding far beyond the territories that should have been affected.

In April 1871, the government decided on a plan to dispose of hansatsu, and recall operations were begun the following year. The removal of hansatsu from circulation was completed in June 1879. In recalling the hansatsu, the government determined the recall value of the various notes on the basis of the regional currency rate on July 14, 1871, the day the hansatsu disposition ordinance was issued. This date also corresponded to the time when the government was carrying out the abolition of feudal domains and the establishment of prefectures. The hansatsu notes were exchanged for currency issued by the Meiji government.

An interesting sidelight was thrown onto the issue of the disposition of hansatsu by Kaoru Inoue, the finance minister at the time, as he was reminiscing about the matter many years later during a round-table discussion:

The abolition of feudal domains and establishment of prefectures was necessary for realistic, practical reasons rather than theoretical ones. It was the only way to take financial affairs out of the hands of the feudal lords. Another problem ... was that there were all kinds of hansatsu floating around—rice notes, gold notes, silver notes, Tenpo-era copper coin notes, four-mon copper coin notes, and so forth. And then, farm taxes were not being paid in kind, but in the hansatsu of that domain or whatever. There was no official paper currency issued by the shogunate.... The shogunate could not very well honor notes from some places and not others. As a result, all kinds of notes from the clans made their way into the Ministry of Finance. Could the salaries of public officials be paid in this currency? To most officials, money of this sort would have been useless.... It was the confusion resulting from this state of affairs that led us to realize we had no choice but to abolish the feudal domains and establish prefectures.

Inoue implies here that the disposition of hansatsu was the *motive behind* the political reform that abolished the feudal domains and established the prefectures, rather than one of its results. Very few people realize this. The circulation of various currencies in the Edo period had reached such unmanageable proportions that the Meiji politicians were forced to carry out a major political reform to bring the currency situation under control. This means that if the circulation of currency had not been as great as it was, the feudal domains might have been retained as political units.

+ + +

In his book *En no rekishi* (The history of the yen), Toshihiko Yoshino, a former Bank of Japan director and authority on the history of that institution, made the following comment: "To recount the history of the yen is to recount its tragedy. What I mean is this:

An overall view of the period since the creation of the yen as a unit of currency shows that the amount of goods purchasable with one of these units has been dropping steadily." As Yoshino points out, the reverse side of the economic development in the Meiji and subsequent eras was ongoing inflation and its effects on the life of the people. This trend reached an extreme with the runaway inflation at the end of World War II. If we compare the price of rice in 1871, the year the yen was born, with today's price, we find that the price of rice has increased more than ten-thousandfold during the last 120 years, as a result of the drastic decline in the value of the yen.

Since the early 1980s, however, a new chapter in the history of the yen has dawned with the so-called high-yen phenomenon. In 1949 the exchange rate of the yen was fixed at ¥360 to the U.S. dollar. Assuming that the present rate is around ¥105 to the dollar, the strength of the yen against the dollar has increased more than threefold since that time.

It is said that "money is a mirror of the times." I believe that the history of money provides an accurate reflection of the economic history of a nation. When the oil shock of October 1973 plunged the world economy into the sudden crisis of a global recession, Japan embarked upon a program of constructive economic measures to meet the new challenge. Thanks to their success, the Japanese economy quickly extricated itself from the worst recession of the postwar age, and Japan went on to become an economic giant, a financial power, and a large creditor nation.

Japanese money today is the product of a historical process that dates back to the Edo period. This process was closely bound up with the financial and social structures of premodern and modern Japan, the first Asian nation to generate a mass currency. In fact, we might say it was the emergence of a mass society and mass currency during the Edo period that set the direction for the economic development of subsequent eras up to the present. Finally, the recent high-yen phenomenon demonstrates one of the results of Japanese capitalistic progress, and provides a hint of the direction Japan might take in the twenty-first century.

Small Factories:
The Underpinnings of Industry

Kōji Miyake

In a small, unpretentious building on a quiet back street in Osaka, a handful of workers toil away on sophisticated equipment. The machines sit in a dirt-floored workshop. Sometimes oil will collect under the machines and trickle out into the road, which is barely wide enough for a vehicle to pass. Without looking at the finished items piled up in front of the shop helter-skelter, you can tell what the little factory produces by the raw materials and scraps (metal, thread, cotton, paper) lying around.

Practically anyone who has lived in a Japanese city will remember at least one or two small enterprises like this. Many Japanese have memories of playing around them as children and perhaps receiving a scolding for running off with some small item.

Known as *machi-kōba*, these small local factories are particularly numerous in Osaka. Although Tokyo, Kyoto, and Osaka all flourished as major cities during the premodern age, Osaka has always been unique with respect to its flow of commodities. The volume of products coming into Tokyo and Kyoto has greatly exceeded the volume going out. Osaka, on the other hand, has been an important center of so-called secondary production, using products from near and far as raw materials for its processing and manufacturing industries. Practically every type of industry that exists in Japan is represented in Osaka, and the city has a much higher number of small- and medium-size enterprises than any other industrial center in the country.

This is not to say that there are no major industries in Osaka. Far from it. Among the items produced there in large-scale factories are chemicals, ceramics, metals, machines, and textiles. These enterprises have varying origins. The chemical and textile industries are said to have begun in the Mint, the metal and machine industries in the Osaka military arsenal, and the textile industry in the spinning mills of nearby Sakai. The first two were originally operated by the government, and the third by powerful capitalist concerns. Set up as model factories during the Meiji era when Japan had broken the hold of the Tokugawa shogunate and was just beginning to modernize, they relied heavily on European industrial "kits"—total systems that included everything from machinery and equipment to foreign instructors. Probably the only areas of industry in which Osaka lagged behind were steel and shipbuilding.

Osaka's bigger factories originated within the context of so-called modern industry, but this was not generally the case with its small- and medium-size enterprises, most of which started out as something a stone's throw from manual trades. Nearly all the smaller enterprises were involved in production of daily necessities for contemporary urban life, or popular luxury items. A few examples would be pharmaceuticals, dyestuffs, cosmetics, soap, toothpaste, matches, celluloid products, printing and bookbinding,

A *machi-kōba* factory making textiles.

ironwork, cotton, hats, umbrellas, cartons, brushes, buttons, shoes, furniture, thermometers, mirrors, thermos flasks, and light bulbs. Some of the original factories turning out these goods have disappeared, but many have continued to thrive.

Because most of these items were deemed unsuitable for production in large factories, or were never even considered in that context, they continued to be made in the small factories. Within only a few years after starting up—or twenty, at most—these small-scale enterprises were dominating the national markets in their respective fields, and beginning to export large shipments overseas.

+ + +

Let us take a look at some of the reasons why so many machi-kōba emerged and developed in Osaka.

The region that would become Osaka was originally the base of activity of Ishiyama Honganji temple, the headquarters and fortress of the True Pure Land Buddhist sect. In 1580, about twenty years before the start of the Edo period, the sect was forced out of the area by the warlord Oda Nobunaga as part of his campaign to eliminate Buddhist military power. His successor, Toyotomi Hideyoshi, who ruled Japan from 1583 to 1598, built Osaka Castle on the site of the former temple fortress and deliberately launched Osaka as a commercial city. To form its nucleus he brought in merchants from Kyoto and from nearby Sakai, which years before had developed into an important commercial center. Soon products of the agricultural, fishing, and mining industries were flowing in, stimulating an influx of merchants from the surrounding areas.

By the latter part of the seventeenth century, Osaka was firmly established as a commercial city. It had become the nation's largest center for the collection and distribution of rice, a vital economic indicator of the time.

The merchants who handled the various products that poured into commercial centers were wholesalers (ton'ya) and brokers (nakagai) who tended to specialize in a particular primary category such as agricultural, forest, or fishery products. Some handled only one item—rice, for example, or kelp. To protect their interests, dealers with the same specialization formed powerful trade associations called *kabu-nakam*a; these became especially influential in Osaka, which came to be called "the nation's kitchen." Soon these associations were exerting a strong influence, direct and indirect, on producers and retailers of the goods they handled, as well as on members of the samurai class and other consumers.

At first the merchants distributed primary products as they were, without any modifications, but after a time they began to process and transform each product before passing it on to the consumers. Dissatisfied with simply moving merchandise from here to there, they discovered ways to add new value to the same old goods. In so doing, they were able to keep city dwellers in a perpetual state of desire for the new goods they created. Commodity values were no longer based on utility alone, but also on novelty and appearance.

It goes without saying that any gathering place for large numbers of people and commercial activities will soon become a focal point for access to information as well. Dealers in goods from around the country came to Osaka with information about conditions in their respective regions. From Wakayama came news on forest and fishery products, and from Shiga and Hyogo up-to-date lines on farm products. People from Kyoto and Nara, meanwhile, were a reliable source of information on traditional handcrafted goods and, most important, trends in consumer demand in these advanced and highly populated cities.

This is how the Osaka merchants kept track of such important matters as where large quantities of particular items were being produced, methods of transportation and preservation, processing techniques, and sources of information. The people who had the best grasp of all this were the wholesalers and brokers. From their ranks came the entrepreneurs who would use their ability to make detailed, competent analyses and judgments from the information at hand to set up their own processing or manufacturing businesses.

Osaka was also an important site for crafts and trades. In the early eighteenth century the population of urban Osaka numbered approximately four hundred thousand people, one-fourth of whom are thought to have been craftspeople, artisans, and their families. Although the accuracy of these figures is open to some doubt, it is nonetheless certain that craftspeople and artisans accounted for a substantial percentage of Osaka residents. The trades in which they engaged were associated with every possible concern of daily life—food, clothing, shelter, and recreation.

Each of these categories was divided and subdivided into a multiplicity of specialties. There were a large number of metalwork categories that included, for example, production of kitchen knives, scissors and tweezers, weapons, building materials, and locks. Just a few of the artisans involved in making a single sword were swordsmiths, polishers, inscribers, hilt-binders, swordguard makers, and crafters of decorative metallic parts, all working independently of each other. We might say that craftsmanship in those days was founded on the specialized division of labor.

In looking back on Osaka's unique development, we cannot ignore the contributions made by the agricultural sector. The areas around Nara, Kyoto, and Osaka have long been known as the most advanced agricultural regions in Japan. From the early years of the Edo period the peasants of the Osaka plains were harvesting one-and-a-half times or even twice as much as the national average volume of rice grown per unit of land area. And it was Osaka farmers who initiated the production of the rice of particularly high quality used in saké-making. (Since the seventeenth century, the suburbs of Osaka have been home to the largest center of saké production in Japan.) It was in Osaka, too, that the peasants' gradual movement away from rice-centered agriculture first became evident.

The livelihood of the Tokugawa shogunate and the samurai were originally supported by rice collected as taxes from the peasants. The amount of tax to be handed over was decided according to the size of the land. In the eighteenth century, however, the authorities began to permit peasants to pay taxes in cash rather than rice. It did not take the peasants long to realize that it would be to their advantage to grow high-income cash crops such as vegetables and cotton, and by the middle of the Edo period these projects were well underway. It was said that the plains of Osaka sometimes appeared all yellow, sometimes all white, and so forth, as large numbers of Osaka farmers concentrated on cultivating rapeseed, cotton, and other cash crops. Revenue from these endeavors helped make the region the most prosperous rural locality in the nation.

In a related trend, Osaka farmers began to put huge amounts of fertilizer on their fields and to use the land continuously rather than periodically letting it lie fallow. The result was greater yields and revenue—which in turn attracted surplus labor from nearby farming areas and stimulated the rise of new manual arts and processing industries in the rural villages.

How did all this relate to the merchants? As time passed, Osaka's financiers and wholesalers extended their capitalistic influence to the surrounding rural areas. They furnished the farmers with seeds, seedlings, and fertilizer, and loaned them processing equipment and farming machinery. They also encouraged them to grow cash crops instead of rice.

It was not long before farmers as a group could be divided into two distinct classes—wealthy and poor. When poor farmers lost their land, it was absorbed by the rich farming class and by Osaka capitalists. Meanwhile, those who had given up working the land came to look for jobs in the city. This new pattern in the structure of agricultural communities was one of the factors contributing to the birth of new businesses and workplaces in Osaka.

One example of a new industry was the manufacture of farming equipment. Until then, the villages had been more or less self-sufficient, in terms of producing their own implements within their communities. This situation changed with the advance of labor-saving methods, and the tendency to concentrate on specific crops. Now the "village blacksmith" was relegated to the job of repair specialist, and the role of providing the most up-to-date implements and machines was taken over by the manufacturing and retail concerns springing up in Osaka.

The evolution of Osaka's present atmosphere and function was completed during the Edo period. In one sense, it might seem that

Osaka imposed itself on and absorbed the surrounding farming villages. Conversely, though, it could also be said that it was the farming villages of the Osaka plains that gave birth to Osaka the city. In other words, Osaka was a city that came into being, and thrived, by transcending the usual boundary between rural and urban communities.

THE SAFETY VALVES OF JAPANESE INDUSTRY

Japan is said to have a multilayered industrial structure based on a system of large corporations and subcontracting factories. This subcontracting system is thought by some to be the hidden strength of Japanese industry, while others feel that it mars the industry's image. All are agreed, though, that the subcontracting factories function as safety valves for the survival of the large corporations in times of recession. Before examining this function in more detail, let us take a closer look at the factories themselves.

There are many different kinds of subcontracting factories. Some relatively large establishments have a direct connection with the contracting company, and the factory is practically a division of the company. On the other hand, small factories with ten or less employees may be "sub-subcontractors," "sub-sub-subcontractors," or "sub-sub-sub-subcontractors" (literally "child," "grandchild" and "great-grandchild" subcontractors).

About fifteen years ago many journalists and researchers predicted that small local factories would soon disappear. Their argument was, of course, that with the sweeping advance of automation these contractors, largely dependent on manual skills, would become obsolete. This outcome has not materialized, however. If the continuing advances in automated machinery had been enough to shut down machi-kōba, the small factories of Osaka would have disappeared many times over by now.

They are still around. It is true that periods of recession, changes in industrial structures, and the appearance of new machines and equipment did in fact cause many machi-kōba to shut down or switch over to different lines of operation—but after only a few years they rose again like the proverbial phoenix, and are now as numerous as ever. This is why, when speaking of

Two *machi-kōba* factories producing
various metal parts. Hon Haneda,
Tokyo.

machi-kōba, people often use epithets like "never-say-die" and
"tough."

What are some of the special qualities of machi-kōba?

First and foremost, they boast an undeniably high level of technical skill. While assembly-line products from large factories may
be fine examples of Japanese quality control and uniformity, we

should not forget that practically all the parts for these mass-produced articles are made in subcontracting factories.

Second, machi-kōba are able to apply greater flexibility to the manufacture of items completely unsuited to production on an assembly line. In large factories all machines, even the newest and most efficient, are used for only a single function; but a machine in a machi-kōba can do several different jobs.

The machi-kōba have also cultivated technologies qualitatively different from those applied in the large factories. Rather than trying to perfect a single operation, their workers are sensitive to changing technologies, and constantly update their skills. One particular factory I know that manufactures a component for ICs (integrated circuits) is simultaneously engaged in making sandpaper. Originally a sandpaper factory, it possessed technology that later became necessary for the production of this particular IC part and the factory was able to make the transition. Incidentally, the workers in this factory are all middle-aged women.

Third, machi-kōba have continued to foster generation after generation of highly skilled technicians. Mass production relies heavily on machines, but human beings remain essential to technological excellence.

The large investment of time necessary to train skilled workers make this an impractical proposition for large, automated factories. At machi-kōba, one of the master technicians, usually the head of the factory, assumes responsibility for training the apprentices. At some point the trainees achieve independence and go on to become master technicians in their own right.

Finally, because machi-kōba do not operate under the umbrella of large factories, they are easily abandoned by contracting companies in times of recession. Although this situation makes their existence somewhat precarious, it is also their strong point. This is because they need not commit themselves to subcontracting for only one type of work and can always slip into a different line when the need arises.

Here they have an advantage over subcontractors higher up in the production chain. A large subcontracting factory attached to one particular manufacturer of textile machinery, for example, would find itself in dire straits if its client were to fall into a slump or close down. By contrast, the small sub-subcontractor factory below it could obtain alternative work from a currently thriving manufacturer of an entirely different product, say construction machinery.

Thanks to the subcontracting system, large manufacturers can tighten their belts and cut down on production during recessions without having to let employees go or suffer losses on overhead. In the event of a slight recession, the contracting company may not be affected at all, and if the smaller subcontractors are flexible enough they can adapt to changing conditions by seeking other outlets for their services. This is how subcontracting factories act as a safety valve for the manufacturing sector.

So far, Osaka has not followed the typical pattern of the Western European industrial revolution, in which entire cities came to revolve around specific industries. From the Edo period on, Osaka has generated all kinds of industries and trades, without any one becoming dominant. The city's industry may seem, at first glance, to lack a center, but the firmly rooted machi-kōba, with their technological excellence and adaptability, have continued to evolve with the times and provide an element of consistency.

The development of this "miscellaneous industry" has been a major factor in promoting a form of modernization and industrialization quite different from that seen in Western Europe. Japan may be a technological giant, but its people demand a wider variety of quality products than can be produced by automation alone, a demand met by the adaptability of the small- and medium-sized factories. As long as Japan, or rather the world, goes on making things, it is unlikely that the machi-kōba in Osaka and other cities will ever disappear.

Japan's Escalating Land Prices

Osamu Tabata

In a 1989 survey by the Japanese Association of Real Estate Appraisers, commercial land prices in Tokyo were found to be from ten to twenty times higher than those of New York, London, and Paris. These figures merely confirmed what everyone had known all along—that urban land in Japan is outrageously expensive.

Collecting data on the price of property is by no means a simple matter. In Japan there is an entire profession devoted to assessing the fair market value of land. Many Japanese profess a strong interest in where land prices are highest or lowest, and how much a square meter of land costs in a particular district, irrespective of whatever structure may stand on it; in other words, value is placed on the land itself. When members of the appraisal team asked European real estate specialists for similar information, they were met with such reactions as, "We don't have that sort of data" and "We don't understand the purpose of your questions," since European property prices are determined on the basis of the building and land combined. Nonetheless, by employing appropriate conversion formulas, the Japanese specialists were able to assemble the data they needed for their comparisons.

Over the past forty years or so, periods of sharply rising land prices have occurred intermittently every ten or fifteen years. Not counting minor peaks, there were sudden upsurges in land prices during the first half of the 1960s and again in the first half of the 1970s. In the former, the economic growth spurt triggered by the shift to heavy industries created a huge demand for industrial land at the same time as the movement of people to the cities was increasing the demand for urban residential land. The subsequent upsurge in the early 1970s was amplified by easy-money policies

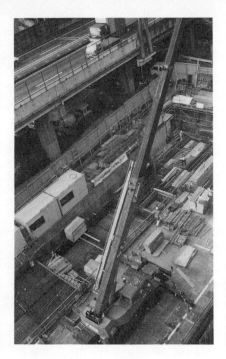

With rising land prices, not only are older buildings torn down regularly but even such less desirable locations as this twenty-yard-wide strip sandwiched between an elevated expressway and a block of high rises have become valuable.

and other market-stimulating measures. Not only did the policies stimulate demand in themselves, but they touched off an "archipelago reconstruction boom" that generated a heavy wave of speculation in commercial and private property.

In the second half of the 1980s land prices began to skyrocket again, with minor peaks and valleys since then. One reason for the surge was the explosive demand for office space in Tokyo and a corresponding demand for residential land to accommodate the influx of personnel. A much stronger factor, though, has been the runaway speculation in real estate stimulated, again, by easy-money policies and by the "surplus-money phenomenon" of the late 1980s. When Japan's economic bubble burst in 1991, land prices dropped slightly but not significantly.

Far from being a recent phenomenon, the pattern of intermittent upsurges in land prices was already evident in the Edo period. According to the records of the Mitsui family, founders of the Mitsukoshi Department Stores, the plot in Tokyo's Nihonbashi district where the main store now stands was purchased in 1683 for 1,030 *ryō*. It had a frontage of a little over 15.8 yards. In 1694, when they acquired land across the street with a frontage of about 14.7 yards, the price had already gone up to 1,730 *ryō*, an increase of about 70 percent in ten years.

Although there are no comprehensive records available to document the general trends, I think we can safely assume that land prices in Edo were rising sharply at that time. According to historian Nobuhiko Nakai, this corresponded to the growth of Edo as a consumer city, a process that led to a large demand for new land development to accommodate the increasing numbers of people moving in from the countryside. In the 1720s land prices fell almost 50 percent when Japanese cities were hit by economic recession, but recovered in the 1730s. Other studies indicate that peak times of rising land prices occurred at the end of the seventeenth century and in the mid-eighteenth century, with periods of lower prices between.

+ + +

During the Edo period, when all land fell under the dominion of the Tokugawa administration and the feudal lords, landownership by commoners was recognized only within a limited geographical range. The rural land system had special provisions for peasant cultivation rights and limited peasant landownership. In the castle towns that sprang up all over Japan in the early years of the regime, the samurai class did not own their own residences, but lived on land formally leased to them by their lords. The practice of private landownership did exist, however, in the districts allotted to merchants and artisans. The land in these parts of town was called *machi-chi* (town land). Unlike the samurai neighborhoods, where residents occupied spacious properties, the machi-chi sections were high-density urban districts full of small residences and shops. The barometers of a plot's commercial potential here were its location and the width of its frontage.

Ihara Saikaku, one of the great writers of the early Edo period, had this to say about using land as a means to make money:

> When you have saved a little money, the soundest investment you can make is to buy a plot of land, build houses on it, and rent them out. Fire is the only worry, but that may not happen for a long time. In fourteen years you will have recovered your investment, and land is a permanent treasure.

Since "houses" here referred to small, wooden row houses, a fire in one would soon spread to the rest. The point Saikaku was making as early as 1694, when land prices were conspicuously on the rise, was that even if the structure did burn down, the land itself would still be valuable.

Privately-owned town properties were called *koken-chi*, *koken* meaning "deed of sale," and *chi*, "land." As property owners, the people with one or more koken in their possession were obliged to shoulder their share of the costs and responsibilities involved in administering the town. This included paying taxes, which in those days were levied on the community as a whole rather than on individuals. As a result the word "koken" came to be associated with the social status of the propertied townspeople.

In 1710 and again in 1744, the prefect of Edo commanded district heads to carry out surveys of koken properties and detail their particulars in charts called *koken-ezu*, which are still preserved today. For each plot the charts record the width of frontage, depth, names of owner and caretaker, sale price stated on the deed, and price per *ken*, or 2 yards of street frontage.

There were a number of reasons why administrators needed to keep track of the land price trends in different parts of the city. For one, it was customary for the shogunate government to claim a house as security from a merchant taking on an official business contract. To this end, it was obviously necessary to verify the value of the property concerned. Conversely, a merchant needed to own a town property of considerable value to qualify for official contracts.

It is evident that for the merchants of the Edo period, land had already become more than simply a place to live and work. It was a commercial tool that could be used for securing work contracts and loans, as well as a means to profit by offering land or housing for rent. In other words, land was a commodity with a strongly speculative aspect, as it is now. Modern-day banks are often criticized for their carefree attitudes about accepting land as collateral, a practice thought to be one of the causes of spiraling land prices, yet the tendency was already visible in the Edo period.

The pattern of intermittent upsurges in land prices is quite different from the smooth curves that characterize the price fluctuations of other commodities. When an increase in demand coincides with a time of prosperity and easy financing, the combination of favorable conditions causes the land market to overheat, and prices shoot up. Increased demand could be created by a large influx of new residents over a short period, or by a booming market for industrial space. This state of affairs never fails to touch off a rush of speculation, the activity primarily responsible for the high peaks of the land-price curve.

Unlike other commodities, land cannot be produced to meet a growing demand. With this in mind, we can define the speculative quality of land as the potential for profiting economically from such operations as cornering, hoarding, and reselling, all three of which are removed from the direct use of the land.

It would seem that present-day attitudes and practices concerning land have come down unchanged from the urban merchant class of the Edo period, with one exception: landownership today is no longer limited to individuals. Now that corporations have entered the picture, their speculative and manipulative tactics, powered by superior capital resources and easy access to information, have greatly expanded the range of land prices. The present situation, in which land speculation has reached outrageous proportions and the price peaks leap off the charts, is a reflection of this corporate influence on the market.

✢   ✢   ✢

The practice of assessing land and buildings separately in Japan probably grew out of the difficulty in assigning a social and economic value to structures. How did people feel about land and buildings in premodern times?

In the castle towns, where the lords of each domain resided,

Typical suburban middle-class homes outside Tokyo being built on 1,000-square-foot plots. When finished, they will sell for about 55 million yen, or US$500,000. 1993.

the castle was the last stronghold of battle, while the commoners' houses surrounding it were looked upon as expendable. For some warlords, the mushrooming clusters of humble wooden dwellings existed for the sole purpose of being razed to the ground whenever the necessity arose. A defending army might set fire to neighborhoods around its own castle to prevent the enemy from approaching. Conversely, the attackers might burn down the homes to isolate the castle.

These military strategies were reflected in the very structure of the castle towns. The ruling lords who built them implemented a form of town planning in which the castle and the samurai districts were surrounded by moats and walls, while the commercial and industrial neighborhoods, where the common people lived, were left virtually unprotected. Thus, many of the town districts were nothing but provisional "dormitories," where people were under the perpetual threat of being burned out of their homes.

Saikaku's statement, "Fire is the only worry, but that may not happen for a long time," can be interpreted to mean that even the townspeople who owned property were resigned to the possibility of fire. In addition to fires set for military purposes, there were frequent accidental fires that spread rapidly over large areas of the town, fueled by the wooden houses built side by side.

It is said that in Edo the great Meireki-era fire of 1657 was followed by 93 other wide-ranging fires over a period of about 220 years. The situation was similar in Kyoto and Osaka.

In 1727 Tokugawa Yoshimune, the eighth Tokugawa shogun, introduced a number of measures to counteract fire damage, beginning with the promotion of plaster houses and fire-resistant storehouses in the town districts of Edo. Since it was mainly the wealthier townspeople who adopted the measures, however, the improvements spread in only a few neighborhoods where people had the means to implement them. The back-street tenements continued to be poor wooden structures that might burn down at any moment, and at no great loss. When they did catch fire, they burned to the ground in a matter of minutes. An area razed by fire was a flat wasteland, with nothing left except roof fragments and perhaps the odd storehouse.

Tellingly, the particular expression for land in this denuded state was *sara-chi*, "brand-new land." It implies that construction can begin on the land immediately—and that is exactly what happened. After a fire, rebuilding would often commence on the sara-chi before a single day had passed. Anticipating fires, the powerful lumber dealers kept large stocks of building materials at the ready, and a construction system similar to what we now call "prefab" was already in wide use by the middle of the Edo period. As a result, rebuilding after a fire was fast and efficient.

It seems that the people themselves were not unduly upset when their houses burned down. In various records left by foreign visitors to Japan in the early years of the Meiji era, writers express surprise at the nonchalant attitude of the "victims" as they went about the business of cleaning up and rebuilding. While certainly busy, the townspeople appeared to find these occasions exciting and entertaining.

Although the new houses were little more than makeshift hovels, they were comfortable and pleasant in their own way, with richly fragrant wood and fresh tatami (straw mat) floors. When people become accustomed to this kind of sensation, it can easily lead to the idea that anything new is good. A new building is good, and to build one you need sara-chi.

The expression "Fires are the flowers of Edo" must have originated in the confident belief that a new town, and a new life, would rise up out of the ashes. No wonder that to this day it is difficult to assign a value to buildings. The point is not that buildings have little value in themselves, but that their relative impermanence means they simply cannot be weighed on the same scale as land, which is always thought of as sara-chi.

✦ ✦ ✦

Even if wooden buildings do not burn down, they deteriorate much more quickly than stone or brick structures, especially when they are of low quality to begin with. Between fires and normal deterioration, rebuilding was an ever-present fact of life in the towns of the Edo period. As soon as sara-chi became available, a new structure shot up on it in the twinkling of an eye.

Today, sara-chi is often created deliberately. Traditional-style houses are ruthlessly demolished. Developers knock down ten-year-old multistoried apartment buildings, and more sara-chi is made. The belief in sara-chi, which stems from the love of new things, is still deeply rooted in the psyche of Japan's urban population. When people buy land, they want it to be sara-chi. Even a lot with a magnificent building on it will be evaluated in terms of the value of land in that district. Thus the process of demolition and rebuilding goes on and on.

During the Edo period, the construction system became progressively more refined. The prefabricated parts were all of standard shape and size, so that people would have no trouble obtaining new parts to match whatever might be left after a fire. The house facades created from these well-coordinated parts were actually quite attractive, but uniformity was the rule. In fact, the feudal authorities prohibited the masses from incorporating any diversity of expression or original ideas at all into their homes. Under these circumstances, the only kind of "new house" people could hope for was a house built with new materials.

Uniformity is no longer the case today. Buildings now use various structural forms, and there are all sorts of methods and materials for finishing the surface. Now that the social restrictions on

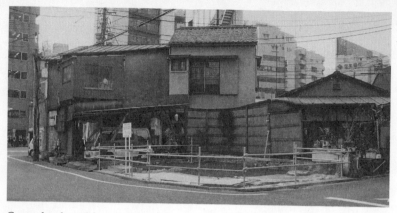

Corner lot cleared for rebuilding. The *sara-chi* phenomenon.

design have totally disappeared, new buildings are expected to incorporate ever-new features and designs, and to stand out. This is especially true of commercial architecture; but even when it comes to residential construction, people want a design distinct from their neighbors', and finishing touches with some originality. Thus, the urban landscape is ever-changing and shows no sign of evolving toward any kind of harmony.

The present age, with its insatiable appetite for fashionable buildings, is pushing the wish for sara-chi to unheard-of extremes. In the midst of this high demand for new land—especially on the part of industry—how can there be any hope of preventing land prices from skyrocketing over and over again?

IV

TRENDS, SOCIAL INSTITUTIONS, AND HUMAN RELATIONS

Gaijin: The Foreigner in Japan

Toshio Yokoyama

In modern Japan, the most common casual expression for a foreigner is "gaijin." It literally means "outsider" and can sometimes take on a connotation approaching "alien," in the sense of someone from another planet. The careless use of the term by those who consider themselves "pure Japanese" remains a sore spot for residents of other nationalities, who now account for about one percent of the population.

The implications of any term used to refer to people of another sex, race, or religion tend to vary according to the power dynamic between speaker and listener. When this relationship is not friendly or equal, any such word used to describe the party of lesser power can cause irritation or bruise feelings, even though the speaker may not have intended to do so. This phenomenon is at work in Japan, where a frequent topic of letters to the editor in English-language newspapers is criticism of the "parochial, narrow-minded" attitude implied by the blanket use of the word "gaijin."

It is well known that foreigners stand out in Japanese society, even in large cities. Japan, to be sure, is a country where skin and hair coloring are fairly uniform, and people whose outer appearance differs from the majority are bound to be visually conspicuous. This is something that happens anywhere under similar conditions. When I say foreigners stand out in Japanese society, however, I am thinking not of their outer appearance so much as the way they are made to stand apart. The tendency to lump all foreigners together and treat them in a special manner cannot help but isolate them to a certain degree. This is why even people from other Asian countries, whose physical characteristics do not differ significantly from those of many Japanese, can still be said to stand out in Japan. As a result, with some exceptions, foreigners tend to cluster in certain neighborhoods, and this in turn reinforces the "them-and-us" mentality of the Japanese.

Some will point to the language handicaps of the visitors themselves as one cause of this. Since the Japanese language does not have the international status of, say, French, German, or Spanish, foreigners with little interest in Japanese society and culture may not be prepared to make an effort to learn more than the minimum required for survival. Such people naturally prefer to live near other speakers of their language and may have few occasions to associate with people who speak only Japanese. On the other hand, Japanese newspapers and magazines often receive letters from people of other nationalities who *are* fluent in Japanese—yet still complain of not feeling accepted.

The following statement by an English fashion model, included in a book of interviews with foreign residents in Japan, is representative of the experience of many transplanted residents.

> I'd go crazy if I didn't use a Walkman when I walk on the street. Wherever I go, I hear the words "Ah, gaijin!" This, from children and adults alike.... That's why many of my 'gaijin' acquaintances have given up trying to fit into Japanese society, and are here simply for the purpose of making money, as models, teachers, and so on. You might say that for 'gaijin' in Japan, it's easier just to float on the surface. (In Zainichi gaikokujin, ed. Y. Ezaki and H. Moriguchi.)

Some feelings of alienation are to be expected while living abroad. The work of trying to "fit in" will necessarily have its ups and downs, especially if the country, like Japan, has a lengthy history and has retained many of its traditional customs. It does seem, however, that the sense of isolation experienced by all too many non-Japanese residents of Japan may take on more serious proportions than elsewhere.

The crux of the problem lies in the Japanese tendency to

Foreign models in Japanese advertisements.

distance foreigners from the sphere of ordinary humanity. There is an unconscious tendency to put foreigners on a pedestal, almost to the point of thinking of them as supernatural beings, even gods. This sort of deification may sound like a positive, flattering view, but being treated as a god can quickly become tiresome. It should also be noted that in Japan's polytheistic tradition, not all gods are admirable. Thus foreigners may be seen by turns as evil gods (demons) wreaking havoc in the native land, or gods of good fortune who captivate everyone with their novelty and beauty.

In some situations all gaijin are treated with suspicion. The "no gaijin" stipulation in numerous rental listings at real estate agencies does not distinguish among different kinds of foreigners. A young person seriously considering marriage to a foreigner is often warned against it by relatives and friends of all ages, simply because the other person is not Japanese. But in the world of commercial advertising the foreigner becomes a god of good fortune. The use of foreign (usually Western and white) models is one of the most surefire routes to wide consumer appeal.

+ + +

By tracing the evolution of the expression "gaijin," we can gain some insight into the historical background of the special treatment of foreigners in Japan. The word itself derives from the Chinese *waijen*, written with the same characters. In ancient China this word meant "person from another country" or, more simply, "outsider." As far as can be gathered from Japanese dictionaries published from the eleventh century on, the characters for "waijen" were transcribed in Japan as *gwaijin*, and the expression came to be used mainly in the sense of "outsider," although it sometimes referred to anyone who was not a family relation.

Written materials surviving from these centuries contain many examples of the use of "gwaijin" free from any discriminatory nuance. It is likely, though, that the word was used only among people versed in the Chinese classics, because it was not to be found in the popular character dictionaries published in the mid-seventeenth century.

Although with the Meiji Restoration of 1867 the word *gwaikokujin* (person from an outside country) came into everyday use to describe foreigners, the shortened form "gwaijin" did not appear until several years later. In the early years of the Meiji era, newspapers often ran articles about foreigners, but the term "gwaijin" was not applied to them until around the mid-1870s, which represents the height of the westernization movement. When the word did appear, it already bore a nuance of suspicion and contempt.

One factor that may have shaped these feelings was that more than five hundred young foreigners ignorant of Japanese ways had been hired by the government as technicians and teachers just prior to that time, in some cases at salaries comparable to those of government ministers. In various parts of the country these foreign "experts" were idolized by the local people, much to the irritation of those who had previously been in charge. It is understandable how a word like "gwaijin," charged with ambivalence, could have emerged at that time.

We ought not to assume, however, that the roots of the present-day epithet "gaijin" extend only as far back as the latter half of the nineteenth century. Beginning in the Edo period another word was frequently used in a similar sense—this was *taryōmono*, meaning a person from another domain. In the administrative ideology of the Tokugawa regime, all outsiders were considered potentially problematic and lumped together under the label of taryōmono. The expression itself dates back to the Warring States period of the fifteenth and sixteenth centuries, but it was probably not until the eighteenth century that an attitude of rejection of strangers gained wide currency among the common people.

The process by which this attitude gradually took hold paralleled the steady escalation of restrictions on people's geographic mobility. In the eighteenth century, when frugality became a central concern of the shogunate, the authorities imposed a host of detailed restrictions on the mobility of people and products, in order to prevent the consumeristic impulses of people in the commercialized urban centers from reaching the smaller towns and the rural areas. In this atmosphere, taryōmono presented a hindrance to policies aimed at maintaining a stable, stationary order, and they became the object of ever-increasing suspicion.

Contemporary travel accounts indicate, however, that the latter part of the eighteenth century also saw the revival of an older, opposite tradition—that of idolizing *marebito* (unusual visitors), or visitors from faraway places. Folklorists point out that an ancient prototype of this can be found in faith in *ebisu* (drifting stranger-gods), whereby people believed that drifters from unknown places possessed spiritual powers. There are also many Buddhist legends about a person being rewarded with good fortune for helping a poor, fallen traveler, who turns out to have been an incarnation of the Buddha.

The resurgence of the tendency to idolize marebito was related to the rise of a newly affluent class of merchants and farmers who could afford to travel. It was not long before considerable numbers of people were roaming the countryside, making the rounds of famous landmarks mentioned in the Japanese classics, or visiting out-of-the-way places few outsiders had ever seen. Circumventing official restrictions with plausible excuses for travel, such as religious pilgrimages or official business, these travelers were welcomed nearly everywhere they went.

One important factor in the growth of this type of tourism was the publication of a wave of travel journals by prominent scholars and other respected figures. With time, their impressions of the places they had visited came to be seen as a reflection on the lords who ruled the respective domains, and these journals became a source of popular gossip.

It was about this time that the strict laws concerning taryō-mono began to loosen up. By the beginning of the nineteenth century, lords throughout the country were impressing upon their subjects the need to avoid ridicule of their domain by travelers, and some were issuing ordinances to promote this policy. Restaurants were set up on the major roads, and castle towns were urged to present whitewashed walls, expensive roof tiles, and shops displaying attractive merchandise.

This eagerness to impress taryōmono suggested that in some sense strangers had made a transition from objects of distrust to something approaching visiting dignitaries. The tendency continued to grow stronger throughout the first half of the nineteenth century, and was recorded by English visitors at the end of the feudal era. For example, Captain Sherard Osborn, a member of Lord Elgin's delegation which came to Japan in 1858 to conclude the Anglo-Japanese Trade Treaty, wrote that "two facts" concerning Japan were "well worthy of note, and should be kindly remembered" by the Christian world. They were "that the Japanese know what foreigners have said about them, and that they are very sensitive to criticism." (In *Blackwood's Edinburgh Magazine,* May 1859.)

Despite the spread of this new eagerness to impress, the distrust of outsiders which had served as a guiding principle since the seventeenth century continued to survive in official policies. This is why the various travel journals written in the first half of the nineteenth century contain many examples of the same traveler being welcomed in some places, and in others refused even a single night's lodging and turned back into the streets. In other words, the attitude toward taryōmono grew progressively more ambivalent as the Edo period wore on. Whether people showed wariness toward outsiders or gave them a warm welcome, the psychological barriers dictating that they be treated specially remained in place. This, then, was the historical situation that preceded the emergence of the word "gaijin" in the mid-1870s.

+ + +

It is only fair to note that the time-frame we have been discussing here is the first half of the nineteenth century, when a tendency to treat foreigners as non-persons was evident in many other countries as well. But the question is, why should this attitude still dominate Japan today, as if it were a valued part of traditional culture?

The standard on which people based the "them-and-us" distinction must have been a durable one. A hint as to what it might have been is provided by the records left by Kauchiya Kashō, a seventeenth-century resident of what was at that time a small town south of Osaka (*Kauchiya Kashō*, ed. T. Nomura, Seibundo, 1955). One of the people he mentions is a Korean woman named Chiyo. Brought to Japan as a captive of Toyotomi Hideyoshi's army following its invasion of Korea in the 1590s, she ended up living on the outskirts of the town, where people called her "Namari Chiyo" (Chiyo with the accent) because she spoke differently from them.

To describe how "truly different" this woman was, Kashō pointed out that she was unclean and grasping, and would walk in and out of people's houses acting "as if she were the mistress." He also emphasized that she did not practice the changeover from lined to unlined kimonos in the traditionally established manner on the first day of summer. To Chiyo, the seasonal change of garments on a single specified day, like the various other annual customs faithfully observed by the local people, must have seemed largely irrational.

I think of the attitude evident in Kashō's account as the starting point of the phenomenon in which foreigners continue to "stand out" today in Japanese society. His is the psychology whereby customs that have neither rhyme nor reason for anyone other than the local inhabitants are so crucial to cultural and personal identity that anyone not bound by those customs is seen as "truly different."

Most Japanese today still adhere, almost unconsciously, to a calendar full of centuries-old traditions involving food, clothing, house decorations, family rituals, special greetings, and the exchange of gifts. Indeed, this very continuity is a prime factor in the stability of modern Japanese urban society. To neglect these practices would be to invite chaos into the delicately preserved civility thought to enable people, gods, and inanimate objects to coexist in harmony. Conversely, provided that a person follows the dictates of custom, he or she is considered a "good person," that is, one in whose presence everyone is comfortable with.

The process of ritualization of Japanese urban life began when the lingering winds of the Warring States period died down in the seventeenth century and has continued unbroken into the present century. Although it weakened somewhat after World War II, it lives on. What stands out in contrast to the experience of Western Europe and China is that in Japan this ritualization was adopted by the masses long ago, and has become minutely formalized. Many of the English people who visited Japan during the last quarter of the nineteenth century attributed their impressions of Japanese people's good manners to the country's "civilization." Another possible interpretation would have been to view Japan as a society under the tyranny of ritual.

Japan has ritualized both time and space. In addition to the numerous annual customs, which relate to time, many Japanese use various methods to preserve an appropriate "distance" from others, including an extreme preoccupation with distinctions of seniority and rank. A further example of the country's finely tuned etiquette of distancing is its all-pervasive honorific language.

Let us take a look at one example of the way this kind of language functions to exclude outsiders who are unfamiliar with it.

This incident is taken from the memoirs of the late Nobel prize-winning physicist Richard Feynman (1918–88). During a stay at a research institute in this country, he made a certain amount of effort to learn Japanese. One day he became confused when his Japanese tutor tried to teach him the various ways to say "look." It seemed that he should use one word, meaning "glance at," when inviting a person to look at his own garden, and a different word, meaning "observe," when being shown someone else's garden.

Feeling certain that such troublesome rules would need not apply among scientists, he asked his colleagues:

> "How would I say in Japanese, 'I solve the Dirac Equation'?"
>
> They said such-and-so.
>
> "OK. Now I want to say, 'Would *you* solve the Dirac Equation?'—how do I say that?"
>
> "Well, you have to use a different word for 'solve,' " they said.
>
> "Why?" I protested. "When *I* solve it, I do the same damn thing as when *you* solve it!"
>
> "Well, yes, but it's a different word—it's more polite."

Professor Feynman continues, "I gave up. I decided that this wasn't the language for me, and stopped learning Japanese." (In *Surely You're Joking, Mr. Feynman*, W. W. Norton, 1985.)

Three hundred years ago, when Kashō's attention was drawn to Chiyo's presumptuous behavior as a visitor to other people's homes, he may well have been struck by the language she used. Given her limited social contacts, it is quite possible that she had not mastered the art of speaking "polite" Japanese.

We might conclude that the tendency of foreigners to stand out and become the objects of special treatment in Japan stems at least partly from the fact that, for better or worse, the core structure of this society remains "too civilized" for many newcomers.

I have already mentioned that the special treatment of foreigners in Japan can be understood as a form of deification.

In this sense foreigners share something in common with another group—the imperial family. There is no doubt that the concept of *tashika na ie* (the respectable household), highly esteemed by Japanese urban society since the late seventeenth century, was a product of a general eagerness to identify with the ritualistic lifestyle of the court. These refined manners and customs, centered on reverence for the imperial family, were exactly to the taste of newly affluent city dwellers. Their desire to imitate that refinement was an important driving force in Japanese cultural history over the last few centuries. This same sensibility prevails today.

But now, as we approach the end of the twentieth century, the development of global information networks and the worldwide advance of democracy have begun to make traditional distinctions between superior-inferior and insider-outsider seem somewhat absurd. These developments cannot help but challenge the workings of the "ritualistic machine" that is Japanese society.

How much longer can the younger generations go on being quite so "refined and civilized" with a straight face? I imagine this same question may occasionally cross the minds of many of Japan's gaijin.

The Wedding Reception:
Old Rituals in New Disguises

Atsushi Katagi

Wedding ceremonies and receptions in modern Japan have been transformed into commercialized shows. Needless to say, the weddings of movie and television celebrities are featured on television and in weekly magazines, but the obsession with showy weddings is not limited to the entertainment world. Spurred on by a plethora of information and advertisements, ordinary people too hold fashionable weddings in hotels or wedding halls, and then set out on package-tour honeymoons. In fact, the bridal business has turned into a trillion-yen industry.

Until the turn of the century, weddings were secular affairs generally celebrated at home. The practice of holding nuptial celebrations at wedding halls and hotels traces its origin to the emergence of the Shinto wedding ceremony toward the end of the Meiji era. Two major factors led to the establishment of this ceremony. One was the example of the Christian wedding, which entered Japan along with Western culture in general after the Meiji Restoration in 1867. The other was the promotion of Shinto as the state religion.

In 1899, the wedding ceremony of the crown prince (later Emperor Taisho) was performed as a Shinto rite in the Imperial Sanctuary, in accordance with the new Imperial Household Marriage Ordinance. Two years later, ceremonies modeled on the prince's wedding began to take place at Hibiya Grand Shrine in Tokyo. These weddings gained popularity among the middle class during the Taisho era. It was not long before Shinto weddings were being performed in eastern Japan at Nogi Shrine, Tairei Hall, and the Tokyo branch of the Izumo Grand Shrine; and in western Japan at Osaka's Tenmangū Shrine, Kyoto's Heian Shrine, and

Kobe's Minatogawa Shrine. An illustrated supplement on weddings in the women's magazine *Shufu no tomo* in 1931 reported that the most common wedding ceremonies in urban areas were Shinto.

The drive for modernization during the Meiji era gave rise to a new class of urban residents—military personnel, public officials, white-collar workers—who were no longer bound by the feudal family system or village community life. Not surprisingly, these people found little meaning in the traditional home weddings that formalized new kinship and regional ties. Besides, their suburban dwellings were not suitable places to hold a wedding. Gradually weddings began to move out of the home setting.

+ + +

Before World War II, the popularization of Shinto wedding ceremonies laid the foundations for wedding facilities run by shrines and traditional restaurants. After the war, a trend toward secular weddings gave rise to new facilities in public halls. The secular ceremony, which consisted of first taking marriage vows in front of friends and relatives rather than in the presence of gods, and then signing the marriage certificate, was initiated by the Tokyo Municipal Hall in 1951. It soon became customary for friends of the couple to stage a reception for them in the same building after the ceremony, sharing the costs among themselves.

The secular wedding was the product of the postwar democracy movement, which touted individualism and disavowed Shinto as the state religion. The 1959 marriage of the crown prince (later Emperor Heisei), however, stimulated a revival of the Shinto wedding ceremony in the 1960s. Wedding reception halls with Shinto ceremonial rooms, operated by benefit societies, began to spring up. Not only did these halls have a ceremonial room dedicated as a branch shrine, but they were equipped with dressing rooms and photo salons as well. Now the entire wedding, from ceremony to reception, could be held under one roof.

During the late sixties and early seventies, when the first baby boomers were getting married, halls specializing in weddings underwent rapid growth. Regular hotels responded to the

Modern-day saké sipping ritual. Shinto ceremony.

challenge by adding areas for Shinto weddings to their existing reception rooms.

In both wedding halls and hotels, reception facilities were the principal attraction, and ceremonial rooms were no more than an added service. As a result, greater emphasis came to be placed on the reception than on the ceremony, a tendency that led in turn to the introduction of new rituals into the reception, including cake cutting, candle lighting, and presentation of bouquets to the parents of the newlyweds.

After the oil shock of 1972 urban wedding halls responded to the competition from hotels, and to the general slowdown in demand, by moving out into the suburbs and regional towns. At the same time, they repackaged the wedding reception as a show, using the latest architectural designs and audiovisual techniques. These halls, with names like Wedding Palace and Wedding Plaza, had exteriors modeled on medieval European castles and churches, or even the White House. The interiors featured grand entrance halls two or more stories high and huge Baroque-style staircases.

In some wedding halls the bride and groom, after changing

costumes, would be lowered into the reception room in a gondola, or descend a Scarlett O'Hara–type staircase. During the reception they might be seated on an elevated stage with a proscenium arch, through which the guests would be treated to an audiovisual "show" highlighting the new couple's movements.

The trend toward showy nuptials has spawned another phenomenon. Christian wedding ceremonies have become popular during the last decade or so, creating a rush to build chapels where they can be held. Copies of New England churches, for example, have been built in several of Japan's highland and seashore resort areas. After the ceremony the bride and groom are taken for a ride around the grounds in a white carriage pulled by white horses, in imitation of weddings described in Western fairy tales and novels. Chapels for wedding ceremonies have also sprung up in the gardens of many wedding halls and hotels.

+ + +

Japanese today do tend to prefer weddings in which the dress, food, rituals, architecture, and natural environment create a Western-style atmosphere. If you look closely, however, you can glimpse the vestiges of traditional rites in the rituals of today's receptions.

What are these modern rituals that have come to be part of the reception instead of the ceremony? A look at what happens during a typical wedding reception at a hotel or wedding hall provides some answers.

First of all the bride and groom, their parents, and the couple who have acted as go-betweens form a line at the entrance of the reception room to welcome the guests. When all the guests are seated, the go-betweens lead the bride and groom into the room to the loud strains of the *Wedding March*. The couple sits in honor on an elevated stage.

After an opening speech by the male go-between and congratulatory speeches by the guests of honor, it is time for the cake-cutting ceremony. A toast then signals the start of the meal. At this point the bride and groom slip away to change their costumes.

Entertainment and speeches by guests go on during the meal,

until the newlyweds are ready to make their second grand entrance. The change-of-costume routine may be repeated more than once to show off the bride in various outfits. Then comes the candle-lighting ceremony. One unlit candle will have been set up in the middle of each guest table for this purpose. Holding a single long candle between them, the newlyweds go around the room lighting the candles, climaxing their performance with the huge candle placed by their own seats.

When the meal is almost over, the bride and groom present their parents with bouquets of flowers. One of the parents expresses thanks on behalf of the others: the reception has now ended. Once more the bride and groom, parents, and go-betweens stand in a line at the exit to thank the guests for coming.

⁑ ⁑ ⁑

Before the Shinto wedding ceremony came into vogue early in this century, weddings had consisted of a departure ceremony at the bride's home, a bridal procession, and an arrival ceremony at the groom's home. These three parts correspond to the rites of separation, transition, and union found in marriage practices the world over. The passage of the bride from one household to the other was publicly formalized by means of this movement through space and time.

Modern wedding halls provide facilities for the ceremony and reception under one roof, making it possible for a single hall to handle several weddings in succession on the same day. Accordingly, the passage from one household to the other is now symbolized by a short walk within the same building, and the time required for the entire wedding process has been condensed to two or three hours.

Because weddings have been so condensed, protocol has been changed to eliminate the tedious repetitions in the traditional ceremony, and to give the spectators a momentary but striking impression of the rituals symbolizing separation, transition, and union. The new rituals that began to appear in wedding receptions in the early 1970s—cake cutting, candle lighting, and presentation of bouquets—are none other than the rites of union, transition, and separation in a new and highly emphatic form.

Bringing these rituals into the wedding reception rather than the ceremony has resulted in a reversal of the original sequence. The cake-cutting ceremony can be considered a rite of union because the bride and groom hold the knife together. The wedding cake itself, however, is an indispensable component of Western weddings. It is said to have begun with the ancient Roman wedding custom of dedicating a cake called *far* to Jupiter, the god of grain. After the dedication, the cake was eaten first by the bride and groom before witnesses, and then distributed to the guests. Far different is the wedding cake used in Japan: a plastic tower two meters in diameter and five meters high, with a small section of real cake in the place where the knife enters.

In a similar vein, the candle-lighting ceremony can be seen as a westernized form of the traditional bridal procession. One of the Japanese expressions for a wedding ceremony is *kashoku-no-ten* ("bright-light ceremony"), since in the past they were customarily held at night. The bride was preceded by a lantern-bearer as she walked from her parents' home to the home of the groom, and was greeted with torchlights upon her arrival. In the groom's house, both the exchange of nuptial cups and the party that followed were lit by flares set up on stands.

The bride left her parents' home and was united with the groom's family, but during the bridal procession between the two houses she was considered a stranger, belonging to neither family. To symbolize her "homeless" state, she wore a white gown, the garment of the dead. It was only on the third day after her arrival that the bride formally became a member of the groom's family, and was permitted to wear colored clothing again. During the time when she was dressed in white—and dead in the eyes of the community—lanterns and torches were kept alight to prevent her from being possessed by demons.

Although there is no longer any need to protect the bride as she moves around the wedding hall, the image of the torch-lit bridal procession lives on. Its meaning and form, however, have been westernized to give birth to the candle-lighting ceremony.

When the bride and groom light the huge candle beside their own seats, the flame is a symbol of their burning love. To emphasize this image, the candle is decorated with a large, heart-shaped metal hoop.

Fire as a symbol of love is actually a Western idea. In the West there have been various customs involving the kindling of "flames of love" and "fires of joy" at weddings, exemplified by the use of heart-shaped flares at royal weddings in baroque times. While it is not known whether the person who invented the candle-lighting ceremony was aware of these old customs, it can nonetheless be seen as a recasting of the old Japanese bridal procession image into Western fire imagery.

The change-of-costume routine, called *iro-naoshi*, began as a visual representation of the bride's death in her parents' home and rebirth in the groom's home. Today the custom has been transformed into a quick change from a white kimono or wedding dress to one or more colorful costumes, and is less a symbolic rite than an extravagant fashion show.

When the change of costume is from Western dress to kimono, the bride and groom may reenter the room holding a single parasol between them. The old Japanese custom of sheltering the bride with a parasol or hat can be compared to the Western custom of covering the bride with a veil. Both practices imply protecting the bride against evil spirits from above. Here, however, the parasol is the so-called *ai-ai-gasa*, a symbol of mutual love. The effect is not unlike the image of an Edo-period courtesan walking along a street in the pleasure quarter.

As the reception draws to a close, it is time for the presentation of bouquets. The groom presents a bouquet to the bride's parents, and the bride to the groom's parents. In the past, the bride would take leave of her parents at the beginning of the wedding. Now, however, the bride usually goes in street clothes to the dressing room of the hotel or wedding hall, where professional attendants dress her up in the bridal costume. So the traditional departure rite, in which the white-robed bride took leave of her parents at home, is no longer feasible.

In the original ritual, the bride and her parents each took three sips from a cup of saké, and repeated the sequence three times. With the modern reception, the saké ritual has been replaced by the exchange of bouquets, a routine suggested by the image of flower-bedecked receptions in the West, and which now serves as the finale to the reception.

+ + +

Nuptials in Japan have not always centered on a bride leaving her home to enter the groom's household. As late as the Heian period, the most common form of marriage was *mukotori-kon* (taking a groom). The suitor would make several visits to the woman, and then go to live with her family after the wedding. The "wedding ceremony" consisted of the simple *tokoro-arawashi* custom, whereby members of the bride's family caught the groom while he was visiting her and forced him to eat *mochi* (rice cakes) that had been cooked in their home. The mochi-eating ritual later came to be carried out on the third day of the visit, giving rise to the expression *mika-no-mochihi* ("third-day mochi"). The act of eating something cooked in the bride's home was thought to have the magical effect of making the groom a member of her family.

As the samurai clans came into power toward the end of the Heian period, they established a patriarchal system based on the inheritance of personal property by the eldest son. This development led to the replacement of mukotori-kon by new forms of marriage in which women were forcefully carried off, given away as presents, or appropriated by those in power to produce an heir.

In the Muromachi period the samurai form of marriage called *yomeiri-kon* (taking in a bride) became firmly instituted, and the accompanying protocol formalized. This wedding ceremony was a secret ritual carried out at night. The bride rode in a palanquin to the groom's home where the "three-times-three" saké-sipping ritual was carried out by candlelight. Like the former "third-day mochi" eating ritual, this act of drinking together from a single cup cemented the new nuptial and kinship ties.

It was not until the Warring States period, when towns were being built around castles, that people started holding weddings during the daytime. It is said that when Mōri Hidemoto married the adopted daughter of the powerful lord Tokugawa Ieyasu in 1594, Toyotomi Hideyoshi, the then de facto ruler, felt it a waste to go to extravagance for a wedding that no one could clearly see. Instead, he commanded that the wedding be held during the day-time so that the pomp and splendor of the bridal procession might be admired by all. Hideyoshi himself sat on a stand along the route to watch the procession, and apparently enjoyed himself immensely.

In 1620, when the daughter of the second shogun, Tokugawa Hidetada, entered the court as a consort of Emperor Gomizuno-o, a procession of several thousand people was reportedly assem-bled to transport the bride's personal effects, including 260 chests of clothes and thirty folding screens. This extravaganza was main-ly a demonstration to show off the power of the recently estab-lished Tokugawa regime. In other words, the bridal procession was a political show, performed in broad daylight to draw a large crowd of spectators. Even then, however, torches and lanterns were used as before, reducing the magical significance of fire in wedding rites to a mere formality.

As the practice of turning weddings into shows became firmly entrenched, the quality and quantity of the bridal furnishings (such as trousseau and furniture) accompanying the bride to her new home became an object of heated competition. When the daughter of the third shogun, Tokugawa Iemitsu, married Toku-gawa Mitsutomo of Owari in 1639, the bride's furniture and household utensils were all of magnificent lacquerware with gold-flake decoration, crafted by master lacquerers in the service of the shogunate. Although feudal authorities later initiated reforms aimed at curbing luxurious practices, the *daimyō*, or feudal lords, continued to carry bridal displays to extremes.

This trend soon spread from the samurai class to the urban merchants, who were in the process of amassing great wealth. It is reported, for example, that Nawaya Kurōzaemon, a rich Kyoto merchant of the Genroku era, provided his daughter with bridal furnishings that surpassed those of the daimyō. One effect of this extravagance concerning weddings was to raise the technical level of the furniture, utensil, and apparel-making industries and to

Post–wedding-ceremony party. Drinking, dancing, and singing. Painting by Shiba Kōkan (1747–1818).

expand the production volume of these commodities. In the Edo period the custom of singing the Noh song "Takasago" at weddings spread from the middle and lower samurai classes to the urban merchant class. It is easy to imagine how the introduction of singing and musical instruments would have given added impetus to showy weddings.

In this way the wedding protocol established in the Muromachi period was made ever more lavish and showy in the context of Edo-period urban society. This process is now repeating itself with Western-style trappings in the wedding halls of modern Japan.

Changing Patterns in Sexuality and Sex-based Roles

Masatoshi Takada

In the 1960s, when Japan's economic growth was in full swing, novelist and occasional singer Akiyuki Nosaka sang, "Between man and woman there is a deep, dark river...." The "river" he referred to was indeed wide then, and the youth of that generation spent much of their adolescence trying to figure out ways to cross it. In the three decades since, the rigid divisions between men and women in Japan have begun to shift and to settle into new configurations.

One obvious area of change has been outward appearance. Women's hair has got shorter, and men's longer, with the result that hairstyles are often indistinguishable. For casual occasions, jeans and T-shirts are now the costume of choice for young women and men alike. Cosmetics, too, are no longer reserved for feminine use—men's cosmetics sell well, and growing numbers of young men have begun to visit tanning salons and the "aesthetic salons" that specialize in massage, facials, and even electrolysis. Encouraged by an array of fashion magazines targeting a male audience, men are beginning to place almost as much importance on their own appearance as women do on theirs.

This is not the first time a tendency toward narrowing the gender gap has arisen in Japan. In the years before and after 1920, when people were influenced by the democratic spirit of the Taisho era, and again in the mid-fifties, just prior to the period of high economic growth, a rash of magazine articles appeared proclaiming the feminization of men and masculization of women.

Going back a lot further, there were times during the Heian and Edo periods when certain manners and customs allowed distinctions between men and women to blur. In the late seventeenth century, for example, when urban culture was flowering all over the country, it was not uncommon for teenaged boys from samurai and wealthy merchant families to adopt women's hairstyles, powder their faces, and wear sumptuous kimono in the hope of attracting the romantic attentions of adult men.

With the Meiji Restoration of 1867, however, when modernization became the top national priority, the new leaders set about to stamp out every last vestige of homosexuality. In the process they placed a near-neurotic emphasis on the distinction between the sexes. The reason for this campaign lay in the government's determination to lead the nation to prosperity and military strength. Men, who were to serve as the military and industrial "soldiers," would be required to exhibit aggressiveness, logic, integrity, willpower, and physical strength—in a word, "masculinity."

The extreme polarity between the sexes encouraged in that period has begun to relax somewhat, but many parents still have different expectations of their sons and daughters. Today's parents belong to a generation for whom the "male sphere" was defined in terms of cutthroat competition in business and industry. The agenda they continue to thrust on their sons is, "Study hard, make it into a top university, and get a job with a well-known company." Daughters, on the other hand, are encouraged to study flower arrangement and piano rather than focusing all their energy on studies. The situation is changing, and cram schools now have plenty of female students; but on the whole I would say that greater academic and vocational pressure is still placed on boys.

WOMEN AND MEN IN THE WORK FORCE

Until about the mid-1980s, the Japanese tended to refer to "career women" with the phrase, *otoko masari no tokubetsu na josei* (extraordinary women, more manly than most men). This phrase began to sound outdated about 1985, when the Equal Employment Opportunity Law was passed. Since then, not only has the number of working women increased dramatically, but society has come to

Women are moving into many new professions. At left, the first female ground crew in Japan. Haneda Airport, Tokyo, 1991.

realize that women with careers are not necessarily either "extraordinary" or manly.

In the industrial world, women have begun to be appreciated for their particular wisdom, sensibility, and homemaking experience, all of which allow them to come up with ideas that might not occur to men. A team of women, for example, was active in the development of the bread-making machine, which quickly became a best-selling product. It was a young woman's idea, too, that led to the production of a tiny scissors and stapler set that sold in the millions and rejuvenated the stationery industry. These incidents are not surprising, as such products target mainly women consumers.

Women's large-scale participation in the work force is not a modern phenomenon. Before the Meiji era farming families, which made up the bulk of the population, were essentially small work teams in which everyone had an important part to play. The same was true of merchant families in the cities. In both environments, women contributed productive labor while also managing the household.

One exception to this practice of shared labor was the samurai wife. She was referred to as *okusan*, a word that literally suggests being hidden away in the deepest recesses of the house. Her role was limited to seeing her husband off to work, and taking care of the consumer side of family life.

With the Meiji Restoration and incipient modernization, samurai and men of other classes began to hold down jobs as public servants and salaried workers. The pattern of their marital life came to resemble that of the former samurai, and "okusan" became the honorific term for all wives.

Even in this period of modernization, women and men continued to contribute equally to productive labor in farming and merchant families. And in the early stages of industrialization prior to the end of World War I, women made up a full 60 percent of the nation's work force. But this situation was temporary. When the men returned at end of the war, more and more people became convinced that it was better for women to stay home; the popularity of this view climaxed during the period of high economic growth that started in the mid-1950s. Except in wartime, when women had to fill in for absent men, the general pattern of the twentieth century, through about the mid-eighties, was for women to concentrate all their energies on being full-time housewives and mothers.

This trend toward a gender-based division of labor fitted in well with the particular industries that flourished in the postwar period of rapid economic growth, such as steel, heavy chemicals, and construction. Oriented primarily toward growth and development, these industries made maximum use of the "masculinity" so rigorously cultivated by the generation of men who had inherited the Meiji ideals. To women fell the tasks of sending their men off to do the productive labor, keeping house, and raising the children. In other words, a good woman citizen was one who contributed to the national effort by taking complete charge of the home front, freeing her husband to concentrate all his time and energy on his job.

As Japan's economic growth leveled off, the emphasis in industry shifted from heavy chemicals to consumer goods and the media. An abundance of manufactured products stimulated a steady rise in consumer standards. It was no longer enough for products to be useful: they had to be pleasing and interesting as well. In order to survive, manufacturers now faced the task of carving out new market niches, which required insight into specific consumer needs. Suddenly women were no longer out of place in the industrial sphere.

With the rise of conspicuous consumption in the 1980s, all industries started to exploit their own links to "recreation." Sitting down to eat became "gourmet dining"; clothes became "fashion." Computers, which had brought an entirely new dimension of efficiency to the industrial world, became the toys used to play family computer games. We might almost say that the large cities of modern Japan have taken on precisely the same flavor that characterized downtown Edo (present-day Tokyo) during the Tokugawa regime. The popular pursuits in the capital at that time were gourmet indulgence, dandyism, theater-going, and frequenting the pleasure quarter. Then, as now, the whole place had the atmosphere of a playground for adults.

Until recently, men were socially programmed to regard every tool of civilization as a "means" to the clearly defined "end" of raising industrial productivity. Now society has entered a stage in which people are more concerned with momentary whims than long-term usefulness. This is why women, who have become accustomed to living without long-term goals for themselves, are able to adapt superbly to present conditions. Ever since they were forced into the role of "okusan," they have tended to think about new products and inventions primarily in terms of the way those advances might make their lives, or their families' lives, more comfortable and enjoyable.

DRINKING AND GAMBLING

"Boozing, betting, and buying" is a rough translation of a Japanese phrase commonly used in the past to sum up men's recreation. The term refers to drinking, gambling, and purchased sex. The phrase is no longer commonly used, as some of the rigid divisions between the sexes symbolized by these three spheres have begun to break down.

The café-bar boom that began in the mid-seventies and catered mostly to young women has brought about a change in overall drinking behavior. For one thing it has posed an alternative to— and thus weakened—the traditionally male "aesthetic of drunkenness," or "drinking till all hearts melt into one."

The café-bar is a quiet, dimly lit place with a sophisticated but trendy decor, where patrons may commonly be overheard engaging in light conversation over their drinks and snacks. The emergence of these bars is changing the weekend scene in the entertainment districts. One sign of this is a decrease in the number of quarrelsome drunkards about. At the same time, more restaurants have begun to offer alcoholic beverages with meals. Drinking alcohol in public, which used to be chiefly a male pursuit, has become common practice among women.

Gambling is another form of recreation that was restricted to men from the Meiji Restoration in 1867 through about the early 1980s. Now, however, more than 20 percent of the customers at *pachinko* (pinball) parlors are women, and within that group the ratio of women in their twenties is increasing. Women have also started to go to the racetrack in greater numbers. A recent survey by the Japan Racing Association found that 30 percent of the women it questioned had gone to the track to bet on the horses at least once, and that 50 percent of the others wanted to go. The time is past when men would leave their wives or lovers behind to go off for an evening of gambling "with the men."

During the Edo period, the situation was quite different. Gambling with dice and cards was forbidden by the feudal regime, with the result that almost no men but outlaws engaged in it. Women, on the other hand, participated actively in a legal form of gambling—the lottery game known as *tomi-kuji*. The notion of gambling as a masculine form of recreation, then, is not actually a matter of long-standing tradition, but a product of late-nineteenth- and twentieth-century standards.

PROSTITUTION AND SEXUAL MORALITY

Prostitution was institutionalized in 1617, when the feudal authorities established a legal pleasure quarter called Yoshiwara in a corner of Nihonbashi in Edo. After the great fire of 1657, Yoshiwara was moved to Asakusa Senzoku-chō, where it grew in scale and developed into a thriving, officially sanctioned sex industry. Pleasure quarters were established in other cities as well. At the beginning of the nineteenth century, according to one guidebook published at the time, there were more than two hundred throughout the country. Pleasure quarters were usually set at the edge of town and surrounded by walls. Their isolation made them seem "a world apart." This sense was enhanced by the fact that the customer's money was all-powerful there, and feudal rank irrelevant.

The pleasure quarters served only male clients, but the more affluent women of the Edo period had their own outlets for sexual amusement. The following passage appeared in a book called *Tōsei-otome-shiki,* written in 1705: "What do you think the theater is? It's just a front for male prostitution! It only exists so that women can hire the actors for their pleasure." This and other sources indicate that it was common for wealthy women to buy the sexual favors of Kabuki actors, just as men bought the services of courtesans.

With the Meiji Restoration, the samurai ethic of chastity and fidelity for women found its way into popular thinking. This development was reinforced by the importation from the West, at the same time, of the concepts of romantic love and monogamous marriage. Suddenly adultery was considered wrong, though only when committed by the woman. Men continued to visit the entertainment quarters and unlicensed red-light districts, and to keep mistresses if they could afford it.

An anti-prostitution law was passed just less than a century later, in 1958. But even this could not stem the rise in popularity of bathhouses with private rooms, which had already begun to operate in the entertainment districts of large cities from the mid 1940s and which soon took the place of the red-light districts. Known nowadays as Soaplands, these were part of the process by which Japan combined high economic growth with the creation of an ultra-consumeristic mass society in which every human desire can and will be accommodated. In these last bastions of strictly male recreation, the man's role in sex became more passive, with the female staff "working on" customers, in a significant departure from traditional sexual behavior with its emphasis on intercourse. This role shift may have helped lessen the gap between the notions of what is proper for men and women. Basically, it contributed to the popularization of new sexual practices which gradually found their way into private homes, and a more participatory role for women in general.

The mid-seventies saw the emergence of yet another form of sexual recreation, this involving a new, more casual attitude on the part of both married and single women toward having "illicit sexual liaisons" (called *furin*), in which at least one partner is married to someone else. It was a time when women were awakening to their own possibilities for liberation, and their increasing participation in the working world was providing them with the financial autonomy to achieve it. Thus it was not surprising that in the arena of sexuality, too, the taboos against women's sexual experimentation had begun to break down. Furin's new popularity may even signal lowered expectations of the institution of marriage itself. Certainly, over the last decade, the average age at which women marry has risen dramatically, and the number of working women who bypass the option altogether has also skyrocketed.

THE MAN OF THE FAMILY

One common pattern of family life in contemporary Japan is for mothers to raise their children pretty much single-handedly, with their husbands providing little more than financial support. Many fathers who work as company employees are hardly ever home during their children's waking hours, even on weekends. The father's greatly diminished influence within the family has resulted from the phenomena of modernization and rapid economic growth that produced the "salaryman" household, in which the father goes off to work for long hours outside the home.

In farming and merchant households, where the whole family worked together, children knew just what their fathers did all day, and often came to develop a great respect for them as a result. Many children nowadays, by contrast, would be hard-pressed to explain just how their fathers support the family.

Another factor to bear in mind is that in Japan wives usually manage the family finances. This is a carry-over from farming households, where it was customary for the wife to control the distribution of food. The practice of depositing salaries directly into employees' bank accounts has eliminated one small satisfaction that husbands previously enjoyed—actually handing over the monthly paycheck to their grateful wives.

One saying popular among housewives these days is *"teishu genki de rusu ga yoi"*—"the best husband is a healthy one who's never home." In other words, it is important that the husband be capable of supporting the family, but not necessary that he be around to take part in it. In a similar vein, an expression used by many older women to describe their retired husbands who just lie around the house getting in their way is *sodai gomi*, which literally means "bulky garbage." This is the term normally used for large items like old washing machines or bicycles that have outlived their usefulness and are now ready to be placed on the curb and hauled away.

Recently the media has started to explore the problems of men's status as strangers in their own homes and the increasing rate at which elderly wives, unable to live with their newly retired husbands after barely seeing them for years, are filing for divorce. It is heartening to note, though, that many younger men have begun to place a much greater emphasis on time spent at home helping out.

In Japan today there are still many sexually discriminatory attitudes and practices that need to be overcome. I believe, however, that after more than a century of tremendous emphasis on gender-based roles and sexual inhibition, we are now seeing a revival of the tendencies to androgyny and free love that characterized the cities of the premodern age.

What's Happening to
the Neighborhood?

Toshinao Yoneyama

Scientists tell us that human beings have been around for one to three million years. During most of that time they were hunters and gatherers with a mobile lifestyle similar to that of other animals. Only during the last ten thousand years or so have they begun to settle in fixed dwellings. This was a development of revolutionary significance, as anthropologist Masaki Nishida has pointed out in his book *Teijū kakumei* (The sedentary revolution).

Soon after the sedentary revolution came the agrarian revolution, when people began to cultivate plants and raise domestic animals. This was followed by the urban revolution.

The history of human evolution can also be examined from the standpoint of social composition. We can distinguish three stages here: the age of kinship ties, the age of territorial ties, and the age of sodality (ties based on neither kinship nor territoriality). These correspond roughly to the periods of hunting and gathering, farming, and growth of towns and cities. Let us look at this process more closely.

As human beings became differentiated from other primates, they established societies based on kinship ties. These centered on the parent-child, and especially the mother-child, relationship inherited from the previous animal phase.

Following the sedentary and agrarian revolutions, agricultural production became the basis of society and territorial ties came into predominance. In agrarian societies land was the most important factor in production. To occupy and cultivate land, it was necessary to plan, construct, and maintain irrigation systems, an endeavor that necessitated some structure of centralized rule. In forested regions such as Japan, ruling authority tended to be scattered in small regional units. These formed confederations, and chiefs emerged as local rulers. Thus was born the feudal system.

In contrast, dry regions were generally dominated by despots who exercised direct rule over vast areas. Both types of society, however, were based on regionally determined human relationships, or "territorial ties," though the factors of kinship and sodality were present as well.

With the arrival of the industrial revolution and urbanization, relationships of sodality, which were neither kinship-related nor territorial in nature, came to occupy a position of increasing importance in society. The type of sodality that first comes to mind today is a person's working situation. The work place consists of a number of complex relationships involving senior-junior and employer-employee interaction, tempered and further complicated by factors of age and sex. Within the work place there may be organizational units such as departments and sections and also various kinds of cliques, factions, and unions, all based on personal relationships. The latter group may include kinship ties, territorial ties (e.g., people from the same hometown or region), or old school ties. In short, people live their lives swimming in a sea of complex human relations.

There are many more examples of sodality—including associations of people sharing the same hobby, religious belief, occupation, or political ideology. There are professional societies you cannot join unless you have an officially recognized qualification, such as those for doctors and lawyers, for instance; and others you are compelled to join when you receive your credentials. Quite a large portion of time is spent taking part in these groups.

In agricultural society, a regional community spirit of responsibility and cooperation is essential to the very survival of those who must work the land together. When people move to the city and everyone has different jobs, most matters of town maintenance are taken care of by administrative bodies. Yet local ties based on cooperation and obligation are habits that do not disappear overnight. In Japan, city dwellers have replaced the old rural traditions with regular communal cleanup days and seasonal events.

✦ ✦ ✦

The grouping of urban households that corresponds to the rural village is the *chōnai*, usually translated as "town-block" or "neighborhood." Architect Atsushi Ueda, in a book called *Kyō-machiya— komyunitī kenkyū* (Kyoto tradespeople's homes—a community study, 1976), provides a detailed description of relationships within neighborhood groups in Kyoto society. He points out that when all is said and done, the groups are little more than communities of obligation bound together by superficial ties, and he wonders whether Kyoto has ever had any communities in the true sense of the word.

It is true that the chōnai have been sustained by a sense of obligation. For example, in central Kyoto it is the custom for a housewife sweeping the road in front of her own house to sweep a little in front of her neighbors' as well. As a result, the streets are extremely well cared for and make a favorable impression on visitors. This is one instance of the compelling force of chōnai customs.

For the Gion Festival held in downtown Kyoto every July, each chōnai is responsible for maintaining and managing one of the elaborate festival floats. Year after year without fail, the residents have cooperated within their groups to assemble the floats and organize the evening events. On the day of the festival procession, they pull the floats through the streets all morning in the intense mid-July heat. We may assume that the driving force behind the continuation of this festival over the centuries has been the sense of obligation felt by neighborhood communities.

Like other large cities, however, Kyoto is now falling prey to "donutification"—the development of a residential vacuum in the city center. As shopkeepers tend increasingly to live in the suburbs rather than in or near their shops, more and more buildings in the central Shijō-Karasuma and Shijō-Muromachi neighborhoods, home of the Gion Festival floats, are empty at night. Slowly, for this and other reasons, the former communities of obligation are degenerating.

Another problem is that modern times have brought a diversification of people's sense of values. Even where the *chōnai-kai* (town-block association) still exists, and there is a recognizable neighborhood group, not all residents continue to place a high priority on participating in and cooperating with community events. There are those, for example, who refuse to contribute their share to the group donations that have traditionally been presented to the local shrine—or object to the association making such donations at all.

+ + +

Although neighborhood groups may be based on little more than obligation, they have at least been functional. When elementary schools were first established in the early years of the Meiji era, for example, the neighborhood groups were instrumental in finding land and helping to erect school buildings. While the propertied classes or bourgeoisie naturally played the major role in these activities, even the common working folk, who occupied rented quarters in the alleyways, cooperated as best they could.

Cultural anthropologist Yōichi Wazaki, who has made a detailed field study of the suburban residential neighborhoods around Kyoto, has pointed out that school districts are the functional units here. The same observation applies to the neighborhoods in the city center. In the latter, the decreasing number of elementary school pupils has led to an overall reorganization of schools, but the old school names have been retained by other institutions. That these names remain in use even today is an indication that the school districts, like the chōnai organizations connected with festival floats, were important units of neighborhood solidarity.

From the Meiji era on, however, the building of schools and most of the other functions formerly performed by groups of residents were gradually taken over by administrative bodies of the city, ward, or prefecture. This resulted in a corresponding weakening of neighborhood ties.

Regional solidarity has declined in rural areas as well. One cause of this was the post–World War II agrarian reform, which brought about the dissolution of the old village communities organized around the landlord system. Another was the financial downfall of many wealthy homeowners; finally, the compulsory nature of community activities was linked with human rights issues and has led to the idea of the right of residence without obligation.

+ + +

The first ongoing settlement that evolved into a town in Japan was Kyoto. Originally called Heian, it was established as the permanent capital at the end of the eighth century, marking an end to the custom of moving the capital each time an emperor died. Next came the castle towns, created by a succession of rulers in the sixteenth and seventeenth centuries: Nobunaga's Azuchi, Hideyoshi's Fushimi and Osaka, Ieyasu's Edo (present-day Tokyo), and many others all over the country. Some towns developed spontaneously as trade centers; Hakata was one of these, as was Sakai, which had been growing as a commercial port since medieval times. Last, there were towns that began as religious centers, including Uji Yamada, home of the Ise Shrine, and Nagano, where Zenkōji temple is located. What sorts of neighborhoods existed in these various urban centers?

The castle towns were under the strict domination of the *daimyō* lords, who often divided them into districts according to profession. Evidence of this can still be found in surviving city block names such as Gofuku-chō ("kimono-cloth shop district") and Kajiya-chō ("blacksmiths' district"). There was also a tendency among town planners to imitate Kyoto—even to the point of bringing in a Gion Shrine and introducing a Gion Festival similar to the original one.

Kyoto itself had an autonomous government during the Edo period. The city was divided into two mutually independent areas, Kamigyōku and Shimogyōku, each with its own administrative organization. Under these were subordinate organizations called *machi-gumi*, which were authentic local communities. The neighborhoods involved in the Gion Festival are examples of machi-gumi that still exist today.

In his writings about life in Kyoto toward the end of the Edo period, historian Tetsuo Aketa discusses Japanese society in terms

A large summer festival (*bon-odori*) sponsored by a neighbor-hood group.

Neighbors gather for a local festival.

of class: the imperial family, nobles, samurai, commoners, and the "untouchables," who performed society's distasteful tasks. As an example of a commoner, he introduces Rokubei, a carpenter living in a tenement house in a back alleyway. Rokubei, with his wife and two children, rented a space consisting of two small tatami rooms—a six-mat and a three-mat—and an earth floor area measuring 1.2 by 2.7 meters. The toilet and well were communal.

The owner of this tenement house was not the landlord, who

lived at the front of the premises, but a kimono-cloth merchant in a different neighborhood. As the owner's representative, the landlord took care of the tenement house, participated in neighborhood gatherings, and was recognized as the head of "one household." Each household was expected to participate in the various communal yearly events, taking on its share of the work and expenses involved. It is evident that for heads of households, social involvement in the neighborhood was an important part of life.

The tenant Rokubei, on the other hand, had no local responsibility. Neighborhood relationships at this level were quite simple, and the stratification clear: one either counted in the community, or one did not.

After the Meiji Restoration of 1867, the wave of industrialization that swept over the country transformed urban life and gave rise to a stratum of poor inner-city communities. Then came postwar recovery and high economic growth. Throughout this time the concentration of population in urban centers continued to advance, as still more rural residents left their villages for the cities.

People tend to think this process was accompanied by a transformation to a predominantly middle-class society. In reality, though, it was only the stratification of urban society that expanded—the middle class increased, certainly, but so did the number of the poor. A close look at the various districts of Japanese cities reveals that there really has not been significant progress toward equality as such.

At present, the places where traditional neighborhood groups, or chōnai, still exist tend to be the old downtown areas of towns and cities, where people live in lower-class, tenement-like dwellings. Meanwhile, the residents of housing developments out in the suburbs are trying to recreate a community spirit with neighborhood councils, sports meets, and seasonal celebrations of their own. The future of regional ties in Japan may well depend on the success of their efforts.

The Origins of
Japanese Mass Media

Takao Yoshii

There is great interest these days in tracing Japan's development as an economic power. Because the emphasis in such inquiries tends to be on modern technology, most concentrate on the rapid progress of European-style modernization from the Meiji era on. They portray a process directed by able, forward-looking men versed in Western civilization. Yet it should not be forgotten that at the dawn of the Meiji era, there already existed a society capable of absorbing the new knowledge and techniques introduced by its leaders—or at the very least, a sizable stratum of people who were able to assimilate new information and transmit it to others. This general readiness to take on new ideas was the fruit of a maturation process that had been going on throughout the Edo period. In other words, the modernization of Japan did not take place in isolated stages. It has evolved continuously from the Edo through the Meiji periods, and on to the present day.

Why were the masses of Meiji Japan ready and able to throw themselves into the task of becoming a modern nation? I believe the answer to this lies in the urban information society that flourished during the preceding Edo period.

Under the feudal system of the Edo period, the shogunate government promoted the creation of castle towns all over the country to serve as administrative centers. The people who moved to the new towns needed something to replace the traditions and institutions of their former villages. The situation called for the invention of what might be termed "town institutions" that could be shared by people who had come together from different regions and cultural assumptions. In effect, it was a matter of establishing a new set of values for the townspeople.

211

Values are born from people's responses to everyday happenings. In the towns, which were of course much bigger and more populous than the villages, news had to be gathered and transmitted widely among the residents before there could be any general response. It was this need that led to the emergence of professional gatherers of information and the birth of mass communication. By sharing their responses to situations, people discovered common values that came to guide their daily lives.

The value system of the townspeople was in constant flux. This is where the urban scene differed from village society. Village life revolved around a single occupation and communal operations, making it necessary to exclude anyone who opposed the traditional sense of values. By contrast, urban society consisted of people of diverse occupations and social classes, living together in a large area. Here, no one set of values prevailed. Instead, the spread of information stimulated the continual creation of new common values. Their temporary nature made these values somewhat superficial, unlike rural values that dated back generations or centuries. In the urban setting social and cultural phenomena would arise one after another, challenging the sensibilities of the townspeople—and each new value thus generated might soon be overturned by the next.

There is no doubt that the collection and diffusion of local news on a large scale was a key element in this process. In fact, mass communication in a variety of media was undertaken with great zeal, and the townspeople eagerly awaited the information so delivered.

The authorities responsible for maintaining the Edo feudal system did not view the creation of superficial values through mass communication in a positive light. Because such dissemination of news often went against their interests, they issued frequent decrees aimed at regulating and suppressing it.

The first principle of the feudal order was the class system. Stability was thought to depend upon maintaining a strict differentiation of lifestyles according to social class. It gradually became apparent, however, that the system was being undermined by the money economy of the towns. With their financial assets, the urban consumers could transcend their class and gain access to culture and education. This money economy enabled mass communication to flourish. Information had become a market commodity.

✦ ✦ ✦

The principal information medium in premodern Japan was publication. The basic types of reading matter in general circulation were word books, penmanship books, manuals on the art of living, and books on etiquette. There were also sightseeing guidebooks, which came to be widely published during the early Edo period. Later on publications listing the locations and products of town merchants appeared, some of which even provided guidelines for making purchases.

In addition to such practical books, an abundance of entertaining publications appeared from the mid-Edo period on. One popular genre was *kibyōshi* (illustrated storybooks with yellow covers), which had illustrations and text on every page. The genre had originated in children's books called *akahon* (red-covered storybooks). The latter went through stages of having black, then navy blue, covers, and finally evolved into yellow-covered books with adult content. Even illiterate people could follow the story lines in these books by looking at the pictures. There were also kibyōshi that functioned as "style books," full of the current fashions.

Some picture books were published as serials. One celebrated example was *Nise Murasaki Inaka Genji*, a takeoff on the Heian-period classic *Genji monogatari* (The Tale of Genji). It recounts the exploits of a handsome young prince called Ashikaga Mitsu-uji, an active warrior and womanizer. This major work appeared in thirty-eight installments from 1829 to 1842; each installment is said to have sold more than 10,000 copies.

In the course of the Tenpo-era reform in the 1830s, which brought renewed attention to official discipline, the authorities forced this series to cease publication. They apparently disapproved of the illustrations, which were based on the inner halls of the imperial palace. Such exposure, they thought, would encourage the masses to look beyond their class, adulating high society and savoring its scandals. Needless to say, from the standpoint of the feudal administration it was advisable for the higher classes to know about the lower classes, but not vice versa. Thus, when a mass publication treated the common people to an intimate glimpse of the nobility, it incurred official censure.

The author of *Nise Murasaki Inaka Genji* used two devices typical of picture books at that time—parody and reworking an existing literary source while focusing on up-to-the-minute content. Because many of the books were simply reworkings of classic tales, they were not highly evaluated as literature. Nevertheless, their satirical, impromptu character was the essence of what people expected from mass-media entertainment.

Another quality welcomed by city people in the Edo period was comedy, served up in a genre of comical books. A typical example is *Tōkaidōchū Hizakurige* (Up the Eastern Sea Circuit on a Shank's Mare), a travel journal recounting the experiences of two residents of Edo as they travel along the Tōkaidō Road, visit Ise Shrine, and tour Kyoto and Osaka. The book chronicles the blunders and foolish acts of the heroes in the places they visit. That it was a great favorite gives an indication of how much the masses appreciated amusement.

The popularity of purely recreational reading matter, as well as moral treatises, stories of religious miracles, and other edifying literature, reflected the diversity of tastes in Edo-period society. One genre aimed only at recreation and totally devoid of moralistic dogma was the "pleasure-quarter novelette." Taking their subject matter from life in the pleasure quarters, these books were usually written in the conversational style used between courtesans and their clients. Not only did they portray the inside of pleasure-quarter society, but they publicized the distinction courtesans made between two types of clients—*yabo* (boorish) and *tsū* (sophisticated). Men interested only in the courtesans' bodies were yabo, whereas tsū clients developed a rapport with the women and were skillful at creating a mutually enjoyable atmosphere.

Class distinctions evaporated in the pleasure quarters, giving rise to a unique cultural form epitomized by the *kuruwa-kotoba* (pleasure-quarter language) of Edo's Yoshiwara district. Because the bright, carefree world of the pleasure quarter was the object of every townsman's fantasies, the successive "Who's Who" books about the courtesans who lived there found an enthusiastic public.

Yet it was not only men who took an interest in pleasure-quarter culture. The favorite form of amusement among contemporary women was Kabuki drama, which often contained scenes set in the pleasure quarters. The courtesans were played by *onna-gata*, male actors who specialized in female roles. Even women who could not afford to see these plays—let alone amuse themselves with the actors—would talk about Kabuki in their everyday conversation. The costumes worn by onna-gata inspired many women's fashions.

Both the pleasure quarters and Kabuki provided special spaces free from the inhibitions of everyday life. In this sense, they were the supreme forms of entertainment in Edo-period urban society. Characteristically, city dwellers would often refer to these spaces with contemptuous expressions like "bad places," while at the same time eagerly seeking them out.

In this society people faced the dilemma of how to reconcile their two contradictory inclinations: toward extreme respectability on the one hand and indulgence in pleasure on the other. Access to publications that permitted vicarious indulgence made it easier for them to manage their lives within this paradoxical situation.

✛ ✛ ✛

News, too, had its place among Edo media. Great importance was placed on gathering and transmitting news as quickly as possible. The principal medium for this was *kawara-ban*, a one-page news sheet with pictures and text printed by woodblock. People could buy the kawara-ban from vendors called *yomi-uri*, who walked around singing popular songs as they peddled the latest news, social commentary, and human-interest stories.

Among the hottest news items were disasters such as fires, earthquakes, volcanic eruptions, and tidal waves. Stories of fires told when and where the fire had started and the extent of damage, and were often accompanied by maps showing their

The woodblock process: carving and printing. By Utagawa Toyokuni. 1857.

locations. Some accounts also indicated where the authorities had set up shelters for people who had lost their homes. A number of kawara-ban reported on conditions throughout the country, using a highly developed courier system to gather articles. The quick news must have gone a long way toward relieving the anxiety of relatives in other regions.

Toward the end of the Edo period, there was much more to report on than disasters. After Japan's long period of international isolation, a great change was taking place. The coming of the American "Black Ships," which threw the feudal government into confusion, was a momentous event for the public as well. It was natural for the authorities to be upset after having maintained a stable rule without any internal disturbances for such a long time, and their anxiety spread to the common people. We may imagine the great flurry of kawara-ban that must have been issued with the coming of the Black Ships. That this sense of crisis on the part of the masses penetrated to the very core of the national sentiment was proof of their readiness to move smoothly into the role of a modern nation.

When Commodore Perry made his second visit to Japan from America, the things he brought with him were featured in kawara-ban everywhere. Among these, the steam locomotive was particularly popular, arousing the admiration of the Edo-period people, who perpetually craved something new and different. The departure of the Japanese delegation bound for America to ratify the Japan–U.S. Treaty of Friendship and Trade was also described in kawara-ban. Since the names and official positions of the delegates were listed in detail, it is safe to assume that the masses had a fairly good grasp of the activities of government officials—not only on this occasion, but in general. The upheavals and military incidents connected with the Meiji Restoration were also reported episode by episode. Clearly, the reporting of news that would merit front-page coverage today was already highly developed in the kawara-ban of the Edo period.

This is not to suggest that the contents of kawara-ban were limited to urgent news. There were also plenty of items corresponding to what Japanese now call "third-page articles," which appear in the society or local-news sections of present-day newspapers. In the Edo period, such pieces fell into the categories of social conditions and human interest. Since feudal restrictions applied to the former, journalists writing political criticism on such topics as rising prices or how official policies were worsening the monetary situation would often use satire as a camouflage.

Human-interest stories, meanwhile, included lovers' suicides, murders, epidemics, the birth of triplets, and innumerable other topics. At one point, when there was an epidemic of suicides, the feudal authorities clamped down on the kawara-ban that had been especially active in publicizing them. This suggests that the news-sheets must have had quite a powerful influence on society.

Most murders in those days, incidentally, tended to be retaliatory. Typical of these was the scenario where a person came upon his enemy after an interval of several years and finally carried out his long-cherished desire for revenge. In the kawara-ban, such acts were labeled "stories of praiseworthy deeds."

Another popular topic was Kabuki actors. We can find a number of articles about the Ichikawa Danjūrō family, which produced generation after generation of leading actors throughout the Edo period. One actor made the news when he was miraculously cured of illness at a shrine, for example, and another when presented with an official award for an act of filial piety. Suffice it to say that anything connected with the world of show business was

News-sheet of Sino-Japanese War
of 1894–95. Headline at top right.

then—as now—certain to draw the attention of the public.

Publications designed chiefly to entertain, some of which have been described above, played a major role in creating the information society of the Edo period and attracted a large readership. The same can be said of the information society today. There is, of course, no comparison between mass communication in the Edo period and the plethora of media devices transmitting mind-boggling quantities of information to today's public. Even so, little of the information given to us these days is urgent, and the amount of material directly related to life-and-death issues is relatively small.

As Japan absorbed European and American culture and developed into a modern nation, newspapers became an accepted part of society. By the beginning of the Meiji era, various newspapers were in publication. At some point they divided into two major types: the "large newspapers" concentrating on written content, and the more visually appealing "small newspapers" devoted to entertaining the general public. The former emphasized editorials, while the latter leaned more toward illustrated social and human-interest features. It was not long, however, before the small newspapers—the forerunners of today's major newspapers—became dominant, and the large newspapers gradually disappeared.

Yet, while newsprint as a form was imported from the West, it was the tradition of Edo-period kawara-ban, inherited by the modernizing generations that provided the basis for the Japanese newspaper industry as we know it today.

Religions Old and New

Shōichi Inoue

Coinciding with Japan's high economic growth period which began in the 1960s, there has been a proliferation of neo-religions in Japan. The Japanese expression *shin-shinshūkyō*, or literally "new new religions," was coined to describe this new wave of religions and distinguish them from the *shinshūkyō*, or "new religions," that were established earlier.

Some of the neo-religions are drawing large numbers of young people. This is a very recent development. In fact, young people used to make fun of the beliefs of their elders and dismiss religion as superstition. After secular school education was made universal, children were implanted with the scientific spirit and a mood of rationalism prevailed. This led to a steady decline in religious faith and promoted what sociologists call the "liberation from magic."

And yet, the neo-religions are now attracting the younger generations. I believe this tendency indicates the anxiety felt by modern young people. In other words, despite their scientific indoctrination, they are looking to religion to help them escape their anxiety.

The neo-religions have a strongly mystical and magical flavor; occult elements are present to some degree in all of them. Absorption in a mystical experience enables a person to escape from reality for a while. The feeling of having come into contact with something mysterious makes one forget the loneliness of real life.

It is not surprising that young people in today's chaotic world wish to escape from reality. Perhaps more surprising is that this desire may even be stronger than the urge to pursue financial success. The popularity of religions with occult nuances, both in and outside Japan, can be seen as a reflection of this aspect of contemporary society.

Japanese are now living in an age of affluence. As far as material comforts are concerned, our standard of living has reached a high level, and the gaps between different social classes have narrowed. In spite of this affluence, the wish to escape from reality has not disappeared. On the contrary, there are indications that it is becoming stronger. It would seem, then, that there must be something stifling about modern civilization itself.

For this reason people develop an appetite for exoticism and nostalgia. They begin to look for mysterious experiences. It is interesting that modern civilization, which generates the wish to escape, also provides devices that cater to this wish—overseas travel, for example, and the occult-tinged religions.

A common sociological formula would have us think that the rational spirit of the modern age frees people from magic and breaks the spell of religion. There even exists the view that the degree of secularization in a society is an index of modernization. While this theory may be valid to some extent, it does not tell the whole story. On the contrary, it is entirely possible that the very modernization we are talking about may also create the demand for occult religion.

Modernization generates anxiety of various kinds. Anxiety may arise from too much competition, or, conversely, from the absence of hardships to overcome. Regardless of its cause, the modern religions absorb anxiety and feed on it. In plain terms, this is a new magic paradoxically brought about by the "liberation from magic."

✣   ✣   ✣

If the formula that "modernization frees people from magic" were always correct, religion ought to have been declining steadily since the beginning of modernization. This has not necessarily been the case. Japan's neo-religions have been mentioned as one instance of an opposite tendency, and modern history contains a number of others.

Take the example of the Christian Church in Western Europe.

The story we generally hear goes something like this: *Both the Catholic and Protestant churches used to have a great deal of power. They were so powerful, in fact, that they sometimes became embroiled in major religious wars. In those days people's faith was incomparably stronger than it is today. That situation gradually broke down as a result of modernization. As people became secularized in heart and mind, the power of the Church declined.*

In reality, however, this is not what happened at all. On the contrary, the Church underwent considerable growth during the early years of modernization. The steady decline that had been in evidence since the Middle Ages was replaced by a temporary period of revival from the late eighteenth through the nineteenth century. Why was this?

The growth of the Church was closely related to the Industrial Revolution. With modernization came improved technologies, centralized industrial management, and rapidly expanding manufacturing industries. These developments were accompanied by radical changes in the lives of the working population. Large numbers of people began to leave the countryside to seek factory jobs in the cities. As the relative importance of industry increased, the balance of the population shifted from rural to urban areas.

The laborers mobilized by the Industrial Revolution were cut off from the folk customs of their rural peasant communities, causing them to feel lonely and isolated. Their life in the factories, too, was far from pleasant. Poor working conditions, wages too low to live on, and the anxieties of city life all contributed to a miserable existence for most.

In the midst of all this, a helping hand reached out to them in the form of the Church. To laborers suffering hardships and loneliness it offered salvation through faith and preached communion with God. It provided a substitute for the medieval folk mentality they had left behind in their villages.

This loving concern was bound to penetrate into the hearts of the new urban dwellers. As a result, the power of the Church continued to grow visibly greater during this period of modernization.

The cities were not the only places that underwent dramatic changes at that time. The transformation of economic structures caused sweeping alterations in the organization of rural production as well. Landowners in this period were engaged in breaking up and reorganizing the traditional rural communities—a process that must have caused great emotional turmoil for the peasants and created uncertainty about the future. The Church reached out to help these people as well.

To summarize, the Church in Western Europe thrived on the anxiety of the urban and rural populations suffering from the disruptive effects of rapid modernization. By meeting the challenge of the modern age, the Church was able to recover from the decline it had been experiencing since the Middle Ages.

+ + +

In the last third of the nineteenth century, the Industrial Revolution came to Japan. Its arrival brought large numbers of people from rural areas to the already heavily populated cities. The same scenario that had already occurred in Europe was repeating itself in Japan. Needless to say, urban living conditions were deplorable, and workers easily fell prey to modern loneliness. Like their European counterparts, they had been cut off from their rural communities and thrust into city life. In the farming communities, too, there was turmoil and a growing sense of anxiety.

Here was excellent soil for the rapid growth of religion. Loneliness, the most potent fertilizer of modern religion, was scattered in large quantities in every field. Despite these optimum conditions, however, established Buddhist sects, such as Hokke, Zen, and Jōdo Shinshū, did not experience any rapid growth during this period.

There were some religions in Japan, however, that did flourish during the period of modernization—the so-called new religions.

New religions had not appeared in Japan until the early nineteenth century. Two of the pioneers in this respect were Nyorai-kyō (1802) and Kurozumi-kyō (1815). Later, new religions began to arise and attract attention, among which Tenri-kyō (1854) and Konkō-kyō (1859) still have large followings today.

From the late nineteenth century on, as Japan transformed itself into a modern industrial nation, Tenri-kyō and Konkō-kyō

Major gathering of the Konkōkyō, a "new" religion established in 1859.

increased their followings throughout the country. Other new religions to surface around this time were Renmon-kyō, which expanded its influence by claiming to possess "holy water" effective against cholera, and Ōmoto-kyō, a prophetic religion based in Kyoto Prefecture.

In the early decades of the twentieth century more new religions appeared in quick succession. While most of them were originally offshoots of either Shinto or Buddhism, they were quite different in character from the previously established sects and operated independently of them. The new religions continued to experience steady growth throughout the duration of the Industrial Revolution.

✦ ✦ ✦

There are a number of reasons why the old, established religious sects did not flourish during the modernization period.

We have already seen that during the corresponding period in Europe, the established Church thrived and recovered some of its lost influence. Yet this did not happen with the established

Buddhist sects in Japan. At a time when there was a perfect opportunity for expansion, they simply stood by and watched helplessly as the newly emerging religions grew. What was the reason for their inertia?

I think the answer to this question lies in the drastic weakening of the established religions immediately before and during the Edo period.

In medieval Japan, Buddhist temples had boasted great authority, just as the Church had in Europe. For example, it is well known that Nanzenji and other large Rinzai Zen temples in Kyoto provided financial support to the Muromachi military regime from the fourteenth to sixteenth centuries. The branch of the True Pure Land Sect (Jōdo Shinshū) known as the Honganji or Ikkō Society, founded by the famous monk Rennyo (1415–99), built up a strong military organization of its own and extended its religious influence throughout the central and northwestern regions of the country. The militant adherents of the Nichiren or Hokke Sect, too, had created autonomous communities in several of the provinces.

These religious powers received their first great blow in the latter half of the sixteenth century, when the warlord Oda Nobunaga set out to destroy their influence as part of his scheme to unify the nation. Among the decisive actions he carried out in the course of his repression of Buddhism were the burning down of Enryakuji temple on Kyoto's Mt. Hiei in 1571, and a ten-year war from 1570 to 1580 against the Ikkō forces, climaxing in the siege and capture of their great fortress, the Ishiyama Honganji temple near Osaka.

Nobunaga's project of unification was continued by his successors, Toyotomi Hideyoshi and Tokugawa Ieyasu. Their success laid the groundwork for an increasingly secular nation-state under the Tokugawa military regime. Headquartered in Edo, the regime maintained its rule over Japan for almost three hundred years. Although the Edo government was not as repressive as Nobunaga had been toward the religious establishments, its policies were nonetheless designed to disempower them once and for all.

An important factor in this process was the propagation of Confucianism. The diffusion of this ideology throughout society—

even to the level of the temple schools—played an effective role in weakening the influence of Buddhism. Confucianism has no transcendent deities. It is strictly a blueprint for a secular social order. In the Edo period, this secular spirit acted as a deterrent to any nurturing of religious fervor.

The repressive measures of Nobunaga and the long-term disempowering policies of the Edo government, then, drastically weakened the established Buddhist sects. Buddhism continued to lose its vitality between the sixteenth and nineteenth centuries, until it finally dwindled down to a "funeral Buddhism," so called because it concerned itself with little more than funeral and memorial services.

In Western Europe, too, the Church came into frequent confrontation with the secular authorities, who used various means to contain its influence. Western history, however, did not give birth to a persecutor like Nobunaga, who was determined to crush the power of religious organizations. Nor, I believe, was there a regime devoted to promoting secularism to the extent that the Tokugawa government did. This is why the Christian Church was never actually disempowered and was able to take advantage of opportunities for revival. When the same opportunities presented themselves in Japan, the established Buddhist sects were already too weak to take on the challenge of responding to modern anxiety, and had no choice but to relinquish this task to the new religions.

We have seen how the anxiety accompanying modernization in Europe spurred the revival of the established Church. In Japan, meanwhile, this sort of anxiety led to the emergence and growth of new religions. What is the significance of these patterns for the present day?

First let me point out that the established Church is fettered by many anachronisms, and cannot easily adapt itself to dealing exclusively with the anxiety that prevails in our times. In comparison, neo-religions in Japan and elsewhere contain few medieval elements. They have been established solely on the premise of responding to modern needs.

In the present day, anxiety is everywhere. We are living in an

Headquarters of the Buddhist-related new religion Reiyūkai, in Tokyo, with offices, prayer halls, and meeting rooms. Established in 1925.

age when economies the world over are linked by multinational enterprises and global communications. As the pace and pressure of life quicken, the anxiety that has been around since the Industrial Revolution is spreading like an epidemic. This is why new religions are also flourishing throughout the world. They enjoy greater mass appeal than the established Church, which continues to drag the weight of traditions dating back to medieval times.

Since the 1950s, in fact, Japanese new and neo-religions have been demonstrating a remarkable ability to win converts in America, Brazil, and other countries. The vigorous proselytizing activities of Sekai Kyūsei-kyō, the PL Kyōdan (Perfect Liberty Society), Risshō Kōseikai, Sōka Gakkai, and Tenri-kyō are well known. These religions received extra impetus from the counterculture wave that swept America in the 1960s. While the older Buddhist sects, too, have engaged in overseas propagation, they have mainly targeted people of Japanese ancestry living abroad. (A possible exception is Zen, the one older sect that has been widely embraced by non-Japanese, but this was due more to Westerners' interest in meditation than to any deliberate policy on the part of the establishment.) The newer religions, on the other hand, have put a great deal of effort into missionary activity that transcends ethnic barriers.

Until recent times, religious movements in Europe and America tended to take the form of Protestant sects within the Christian fold. In the last few decades, however, neo-religions and quasi-religious movements have been springing up all over the world. Japan has been in the vanguard of this trend. One reason for this is that traditional religions were weakened much earlier in Japan than in the West. Could another reason be that modern anxiety has been particularly acute among the Japanese?

V

THE JAPANESE CITY

The Manga City

Günter Nitschke

The model mirror of urban events in modern-day Japan can be found in *manga* magazines, which constitute the most common and most basic "reading" material for both youngsters and adults alike. Every week, in fact, newsstands and bookshops display a new collection of manga—all aimed at different age and social groups from schoolchildren and young adults to women, salarymen, or sports fans. They are read avidly in the home and while commuting by train or bus.

The translation of manga as "comics" does not do justice to this "literary" phenomenon because their contents range from comic strips, ordinary life stories, home dramas, futuristic horror stories, or outright grotesque themes, to sadomasochism and blatant pornography.

The Japanese word "manga" appears to have been coined by Hokusai, the renowned woodblock artist of the nineteenth century. Manga, meaning "cartoon," is often written in *hiragana* syllabic script. When written in Chinese script, it is a compound of two characters: *man*, meaning "involuntary, in spite of oneself" or "morally corrupt," and *ga*, meaning "picture."

To look for the origins of manga in Japanese history is akin to looking for the roots of humor and caricature. Forerunners may be found in various picture scrolls from the Kamakura period onward. Some examples are the *Jigoku zoshi*, or "Hell Scrolls," the *Gaki zoshi*, or "Hungry Ghost Scrolls," the *Yamai zoshi*, or "Disease Scrolls," humorous Zen pictures (such as those by Hakuin or Sengai), and, most important, the *ukiyo-e* woodcuts of the "floating world," which are based on the popular culture and humor of the Edo period.

The fractured space of a *manga* comic book. From "Adel," by Mariko Shimamine.

Today, manga exhibit a creative energy similar to that of Japan's big urban centers, which are often chaotic with the potential to explode in yet new, uncharted dimensions. They reflect the collective intelligence of uncountable disciplines, and the myriad aspirations of ordinary citizens.

Manga do not need to be taken seriously as literature, however, and unlike literature and architecture, they are not high culture, but "mass" culture.

Even though they are Japanese, some of the characters in manga have northern European faces and blond hair. Just as the traditional Japanese Noh mask changes reality, so the manga "mask" can alter an image or depict an ideal.

Manga also constitute a kind of "throwaway literature," similar to the present-day throwaway "mask" of much of Japan's urban architecture. Manga are material for quick consumption, for speed reading. According to Frederik L. Schodt, author of *Manga! Manga! The World of Japanese Comics*, a 320-page manga can be read in twenty minutes. That is an average of 3.75 seconds per page.

As such, it offers a parallel with the fast cycle of change and consumption in what I call the "manga city."

The manga city is not Disneyland, with its nice nostalgic, reduced-scale, surreal cliches of foreign lands that possess no relation to natural topography or indigenous manmade places. Neither is it Post-Modern architecture, with its formal and spatial quotations scavenged from any time or region from the body of world architecture, or with its claim to seriousness, respectability, and longevity. The manga city is a highly competitive, efficient, and short-lived Japanese urban scenario, quickly constructed or quickly torn down as the need arises. It is as real as the stories depicted in the manga magazines. Indeed, leafing through the pages of a manga is very much like going downtown.

+ + +

While books are stored, manga aren't. Or at least not the weekly editions of them. These are simply tossed out after consumption, or stacked up and eventually exchanged for a package of pocket tissues when recycled. Visual tricks or themes of today may not be fashionable tomorrow, or they may be reintroduced as retro images and recycled into the general stream of popular culture. The same holds true for the flimsy mask or interior "clip-on" design of many buildings. What was a traditional pickle store one month may well be a Häagen-Dazs ice-cream parlor the next. Love hotels refurbish the trendy and often grotesque interiors of their rooms approximately once every three years so as to retain the patronage of their clients.

+ + +

In terms of depiction, anything goes in manga. Likewise, the designer in the manga city can let go creatively, experiment freely, and remove the repressions and violence wrought by pedigree architecture on urban space. In this sense, the manga city is the living counterpart, first to the dead and anonymous façades of so-called intelligent office architecture, often designed by "world-famous" architects; and second, to the sterile, concrete box setting of all modern housing schemes (without exception) in new suburban areas or at the fringes of large Japanese cities. It is the antidote to the serious ego trips of modern architects who are commissioned to build the city halls, museums, and stadiums for the same manga city.

The relationship of downtown manga space to downtown office space can be compared with that of the no-holds-barred striptease shows allowed by law to the soft-porn cinemas right next door, showing heavily censored films. Living in the manga city, as opposed to living in the planned environment of standard apartments or condominiums, is like staying in a love hotel as opposed to an international hotel. In the former, you might have a choice of a room fitted out as a traditional tea parlor, Madame Pompadour's bedroom, a doctor's office, a chamber of horrors, or a Nazi torture cell, to mention just a few of the fantasies available on an unlimited menu. As far as the international hotels are concerned, the Osaka Hilton is spatially as boring as the Berlin Hilton.

Nevertheless, there are some signs of hope even amid the worst cases of visual deprivation and regimentation. In the new housing schemes, some bits and pieces of the manga city spring up in the form of pachinko parlors, twenty-four-hour convenience stores, and the ubiquitous vending machines. The accepted visual and social laws can be violated in a planned zone much as growth of a benevolent tumor may invade a pristine body.

+ + +

The Japanese written script is uniquely suited for use in manga, as well as for the large billboards that appear everywhere in the cities. Apart from its obvious pictorial character, it can be run from right to left or vertically from left to right, a versatility perfectly suited to the ever-changing needs of the manga city.

Not surprisingly, the Sino-Japanese character itself is often used as a manga, its elements graphically enlarged and emphasized. The *kanji* ideogram, presenting an array of ideas in most cases, is the smallest manga invented by man. The kanji equivalent of the word "busy," for example, is a combination of the ideas of "death" and "heart," both of them represented by a pictograph. When used in a manga, the image, and thus the meaning for "busy," becomes: "When your heart is dead and not in play, you are busy."

In the unpredictable disposition of individual events in space, the multitude of lines employed, the audacious speed of the actual brush strokes, and the combination of ideogram with picture, the manga is an extension of Sino-Japanese calligraphy, the supreme art of the black-and-white line. It is probably not due to economics alone that most manga today are printed in monochrome, on non-glossy paper, and with only an occasional introductory page in color.

+ + +

The efficacy of manga has been embraced by government and local city administrations alike in their efforts to communicate with their citizens. New city ordinances, such as the latest Comprehensive Development Law of Kyoto, are publicized in manga form with short explanatory text. So too are changes in national tax laws or measures for evacuation in case of natural disasters. There are manga that teach foreign languages, history, and Einstein's Theory of Relativity. In style and content, manga dominate advertising, telecommunications, and architecture. "Manga-ese" may very well be the new language for the new "information era."

The only limiting factor in manga is the rectangular spread of two pages. Similarly, the spatial limitation of the Japanese city is a fixed grid of streets, with height limitations for buildings only in the two ancient capital cities of Kyoto and Nara.

An important structural feature of the Japanese city is the small size of its individual parcels of property. The smaller the plot, the greater the stimulus to and freedom of individual entrepreneurship, growth, and renewal. As for the distribution of urban functions and the renewal of individual elements, one can find in the small-scale fragmentation of the East Asian city one of the most efficient urban forms for a society based on late-twentieth-century capitalism and rapid change.

Within the limited page framework of the manga, as well as within the limited plot framework of the Japanese city, your fantasy and your finances are your limits. This is the new reality of

236

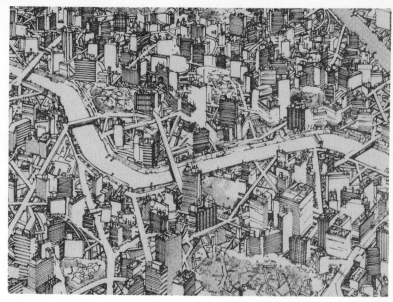

Tokyo of the future depicted in *manga* form. By Sumiko Imari.

Tokyo cityscape, 1993.

Japanese "literature" and "architecture." It is playful. It is part of an urban theater. The criteria is performance, not fixed and canonized aesthetics; at least, not traditional ones, neither Western nor Eastern.

In manga there are major, often arbitrary spatial subdivisions, and within these divisions can be found an abundance of minute detail and variety. In the manga city, urban highways and large-scale "pencil-thin" skyscrapers create a similar, visually arbitrary, structural division over the city as a whole.

The infill reveals a maze of subspaces and attention to human scale, in both the inhabited quarters and the entertainment districts. Indeed, the density and complexity of detail in the Japanese inner urban sphere has no equal in the Western world. This even holds true for Kyoto, where the major spatial subdivision is a clear rectangular one, derived from Chinese planning principles. But the side streets and subspaces of Kyoto are Japanese. That is to say, they are mazes of structural, functional, and visual complexity that defy description.

One double-page spread of a manga might present a situation in which we are simultaneously inside the heads of two different people as they sit in an airplane looking down over Tokyo. This "split-screen" technique of pulling apart and reconstructing perception is achieved to a degree that only gods and amoebas could experience at the same instant in time. Equally, the manga-space city pulls one along sequentially, as well as in synchronistic, multimedia jerks, as if we were moving from one stage set to another.

In manga and cityscape alike, the "new visual generation" is exposed to a treat of the left and right sides of the brain simultaneously: to a stimulation of its verbal, discursive, and deductive as well as its spatial, holistic, and intuitive faculties. Not even the wildest designs of contemporary architects can compete in terms of structural, functional, and visual complexity and stimuli with an existing vernacular streetscape of the present manga city.

The Japanese city is not a collage, since any collage would still be the result of a conscious act of overall composition, even if it were for shock or cacophonous purposes. The present fragmented townscape in Japan is a direct result of disparate wills designing their own work or living spaces to suit their own needs regardless of what their neighbors may have built, creating a fragmented social reality.

In *Architectural Design*, Aldo Rossi says: "In a public city tolerance of the private is at a minimum." The present-day Japanese city defies this statement. In Japan, we see the freedom of individual expression in each plot of land, and a tolerance for the private at a maximum.

+ + +

Manga are dominated by females—by the admiration for and conquest of the woman. So is the manga city. No one downtown pays any attention to salarymen, but rather it is the OLs (office ladies) who are to be seen. Even though women may not appear, for example, in the male manga magazine world of the baseball game, the question arises as to who is imagined to be cheering on the sidelines. If there is a manga hero, there will always be a desired "cheerleader."

The heroines in the popular women's comics look like Western fashion models, with long legs and big eyes. Often, they also appear to be taller than their male counterparts, portraying an ideal rather than a factual image. Urban space in the manga city is just as dominated by the promenading young Japanese woman in her manga-perfect makeup and dress, and the latest fashions and accessories are prominently displayed in boutiques all over town.

It may not be far from the truth to estimate that 90 percent of the "love" encounters in manga involve male fantasies of domination and female exploitation. Does this reflect the way the Japanese male population thinks of love and sex? Or is contemporary Japanese culture merely substituting violence for sexuality?

Manga indulge in numerous fantasies of violence. Apart from straightforward fights among samurai, there are explicit depictions of limbs being severed, heads rolling, and blood gushing. The relationship between visual expressions of violence, pornography, and sado-masochism in manga, and sexual suppression in society, is a complex one. Joanna Russ is probably correct in assuming in *Magic Mommas, Trembling Sisters, Puritans & Perverts*

(The Crossing Press, Trumansburg, N.Y., 1985) that "sexual fantasy materials are like icebergs; the one-tenth that shows above the surface is no reliable indicator of the size and significance of the whole thing."

On the most obvious level, the manga in this context provide a display of the most primary of all human conflicts for domination, the battle of the sexes. On a slightly deeper level, the "male fantasies as a precondition for it, or as a cue to it, are attempts to partly undo the violence in the 'respectable' part of the culture, where violence has been substituted for sexual enjoyment."

The thought here is of the millions of dark-suited, white-shirted (and highly taxed) Japanese salarymen on their daily morning and evening travels, to and from their lifelong imprisonment in highly regimented, pyramidal corporate structures, all of them reading manga. By becoming absorbed in these fantasies of violence and rape, they may very well feel that something of their own identity is salvaged.

On an even deeper level, reading this type of manga may perform the role of releasing the repressed passions in the male subconscious, his actual frustration with the domination, in a sense, of the woman in the real Japanese culture of today. Finally, immersion in the sadomasochistic type of manga offers the attractive illusion of freedom from responsibility and hence, freedom from the burdens of being an individual.

Visually, the manga city is also far removed from expressions of politeness, mutual respect, or attempts at harmony found in normal urban interactions. Its violent alteration of the standard urban fare is a direct expression of the striving for survival of private interests; every "mask" is trying to outdo its neighbor in a highly competitive overall setting. In the modern visual arena, the combatants do not fight with swords or armor, but with pictorial fantasies, images, and messages.

✦ ✦ ✦

What draws the reader along on a journey through a manga is a series of disconnected scenes and images, jumping in scale and intensity, comparable to the sequence of visions experienced on a

Kirin Plaza Building, Osaka.

psychedelic trip. Their visual logic is similar to that used in Japanese television commercials and video games and even the traditional Japanese stroll garden, which employs a circuitous route designed to provide an element of curiosity and discovery.

The same is true for the visual field along downtown streetscapes in Japan, except that they were not designed per se. Their unifying principle is *michiyuki*, or "walking ahead with one's eyes," along a certain stage setting.

The *kaiwai*, or inner urban cluster, is structured around the michiyuki principle. The kaiwai rarely has a single core or a clear boundary but displays a soft and expandable edge. It is an area explored by strolling around certain routes.

Kaiwai are also characterized by the existence of "stop-places," small urban niches where people tend to gather or stop for a chat. They are not planned, as are the marketplaces, squares, or piazzas in European cities, but appear spontaneously at some point in the life history of a particular kaiwai and may disappear at another

Osaka—"The *Manga* City."

time. A stop-place may be just an indentation or recess at a particular place along a route, or an unusual "mask" treatment of a building fronting onto it. This alone may invite a halt in a stroll which would otherwise be passed by in the daily rush.

In the one-kilometer kaiwai of Shinsaibashi in Osaka, the most obvious stop-space has been created by a bridge over the Dotonbori canal. The confluence of various side streets, or branch kaiwai, results in an urban place with a tantalizingly manga masquerade, unique in Japan. "Where are the buildings?" one could ask.

Shin Takamatsu is probably the only living Japanese architect who could design a piece of architecture that blends perfectly into one of the corners of this manga stop-space. The Kirin Plaza Building with all its metallic glitz and Star Wars decor is more of a surreal stage set, evoking in its decor some kind of science-fiction fantasy, than a building providing interior spaces of any great practical use. At night, this manga building becomes a grand urban lantern for Osaka's most attractive urban spot.

With a few more spaces like the Kirin building, Osaka would be the perfect manga city. If we were to throw in a few additional fragments of urban mass culture—maybe a dockside open-air stage for live performances of a Madonna or Michael Jackson, and perhaps a modern version of a shrine to Ebisu, the God of Business and Prosperity—one could not imagine a better manga space. It would be a modern space, very Japanese urban, but stretching back to Edo times with its lively shopping arcades, amusement quarters, or activity districts.

Imagine them pasted together with all the imagery and technique evident in the very reading material of the Japanese of all ages of today—the manga. Surely it is no accident that such a climax of urban mass culture and energy should occur in Tokyo and Osaka, the most commercial of all Japanese centers.

The "Mass City"

Atsushi Ueda

Around the world, in different languages, many of the terms coined in the past to describe the phenomenon "city" had a decidedly religious nuance. The English word "city" was used in the early Middle Ages to denote an urban area large enough to merit a bishop's seat. In China, with its tradition of ancestor worship, the term used refers to "a place with an ancestral mausoleum." And Japan's *miyako*, though no longer current, is the country's oldest word for city. It meant the dwelling-place of an "exalted personage," and was most often used to refer to the capital, where the deified emperor lived. Yet the reality of the modern city has changed so drastically over the centuries—shifting from its former "god-centeredness" to a form almost completely secular—that it seems time we came up with a new word or phrase. As an alternative I would suggest the term "mass city."

This phrase would refer to a city of the masses, which has either lost its religious orientation or never had one.

Most cosmopolitan cities today would fit this description. Modern London and Paris are good examples, as are Tokyo, Osaka, Kyoto, and all the largest cities in Japan.

This kind of city is not dominated by any transcendent personages, and does not have a shrine or castle as its central feature. It is more likely to trace its origins—at least in relatively recent times—to the marketplace than to sacred ground. Its earliest prototypes are the seaport and desert oasis, both capable of drawing in large numbers of people without benefit of religious stability, offering other riches instead. Residents converge in such places from a variety of locales and backgrounds. They are not bound by common ancestry, blood, myth, religion, or fraternal organizations.

In other words, mass cities represent the antithesis of most of the ancient cities of both East and West which, by definition, were founded on aristocracies.

Japan's cities fit this pattern long before the major European cities did. Kyoto effectively became a mass city as early as the tenth century, while nearly all other large cities in Japan were deliberately shaped to this form in the seventeenth century. By contrast, it was not until the eighteenth century that London and Paris underwent similar processes of secularization.

HOME TO THE GODS, HOME TO HUMAN BEINGS

We might pause here to consider the mass dwelling group in terms of its opposite, the community centered on an aristocracy. Just who took on the status of elite in this kind of group? Originally, it was those who served as priestesses or priests, the intermediaries who made offerings to and received oracles from the gods. This role was eventually commercialized, and then stratified into the social class that became the aristocracy. Aristocratically-based dwelling groups all looked to a god or gods; the typical ancient city was centered on a temple or sanctuary of some sort, and served as a "home to the gods."

Why did the groups with aristocracies need gods? Many different answers could be offered to this question. I would suggest that this system of organization arose in regions where a stable food supply was not readily available. Cultivation of crops in such a region would require the long-term commitment of a reasonably large number of families living and working as a group. Belief in gods was a means both to attract people and keep them together. Once established, the divine presence could continually be invoked to prevent the population's dispersal. Individuals were probably inclined to wander away from areas particularly harsh in topography or climate, or troubled by invasion from outside. But their dispersal, despite any short-term benefits, would tend to raise the death rate over the long-term. Supplying the people with a sense of unity would thus become a matter of life or death. A god whose existence transcended that of humans would directly meet this need. The receipt of oracles would then serve as a means of regularly reinforcing group solidarity. It may be no coincidence that shrines and other holy places were often located on a slight hill, or acropolis, rising above a vast plain. In this way, the holy place most likely served as a visual reminder of the reason to stay.

Mass dwelling groups, on the other hand, grow up naturally in places where people gravitate of their own accord, attracted by rich food supplies. Again, the prototype would be the seaport or desert oasis. Here travelers and merchants come and go, markets are held, information abounds; there is no need or place for gods. This is a "home to human beings."

Human cities have evolved along these two distinct lines, of dwelling groups that function as home to the gods and home to people.

Of the two, it is the aristocratically-based groups that have historically given rise to the more influential civilizations. Priests and priestesses turned aristocrat controlled not only the oracles but also the stock of foodstuffs that needed to be carefully regulated if the supply were to remain stable. Rulers then emerged from out of this noble stratum. The most powerful went on to become kings or queens, forming nations that encompassed greater territory. As this kind of home to the gods thrived and grew, the necessarily smaller homes to human beings—where the flow of food was free and needed no special controls—were outranked.

This pattern testifies to the tremendous power of "gods" to disseminate information. When gods are inserted into the communication process, "person-to-person" transmission becomes "person-god-person" transmission. The god acts as an amplifier, projecting vast quantities of information across the boundaries of territory and race. In this sense, we might call the gods an early form of "mass media."

Mass dwelling groups, on the other hand, dependent as they were on direct person-to-person transmission, or "mini-communication," had a greatly reduced capacity for disseminating information.

People fear their gods. Once they give themselves over to belief in a transcendent, awesome being, they tend to accept whatever it might say. The same level of trust does not, of course, exist in the mini-communication that occurs between human beings. This difference helps account for the gap between the fortunes of the two kinds of dwelling group in early times.

Throughout history, aristocratically-based dwelling groups have evolved into cities, and seaports and oases into large towns. There are few examples of any mass dwelling group having gone on to become the capital city of a nation.

The situation changed little by little as civilization continued to develop. Access to paper, to the written word, and to formal education dramatically widened the scope of person-to-person communication. China provides a good early example of this phenomenon. There paper and a writing system were invented in ancient times, with the result that the "mass media" of religion made only nominal inroads. Religious impulse went little further than ancestor worship. Not only did the world religions like Christianity and Islam fail to make any headway in China, but even Buddhism's influence was not decisive.

The invention of printing was another epochal factor in the development of communication independent of divine authority. Bibles spread throughout the Christian world, for example, allowing believers to perceive gaps between the words in the scripture and the pronouncements of bishops. As a result, large groups of Catholics broke away from the Catholic Church to form Protestant sects. This course of events had an immediate effect on the structure of cities. The Catholic city, traditionally built around a cathedral facing onto a large square, gave way to the new-style Protestant form, in which the square was hemmed in on all sides by the city hall, guildhalls, and other landmarks of bureaucratic and commercial activity. As these cities grew into industrial centers, their power to conduct information increased, and cities began to draw away from the gods. In London from about 1536, for example, one monastery after another was disbanded, and their buildings taken over by the silk and other industries. By the mid-eighteenth century, the last of London's city walls and gates had been torn down.

In Paris too the French Revolution effectively destroyed the power of the Church, bringing down the city walls and gates.

Mass cities can be born when these symbols of authority are destroyed, and people are able to enter and leave the area freely. The eighteenth century saw the transformation of both London and Paris into mass cities. Other European communities soon followed suit. In the nascent, and especially the larger, cities in America, churches and town squares had little social significance to start with, and there were never, of course, any city walls or gates. America's were mass cities from the outset.

Japan became secularized long before Europe. The country was first civilized with the Buddhism imported from the Chinese continent in the seventh century. In the Asuka capital, the area in front of the gate of the Hokoji Temple served as the town square. But in the construction of Naniwa and subsequent capitals, imperial authority came to take precedence over religious authority. Though the Japanese considered the emperor a kind of god, in keeping with the Chinese teachings on the "Son of Heaven," the Heian capital, or present-day Kyoto, was built without any city walls. It also seems that people were free to come and go as they pleased. From the tenth century on, commerce and industry thrived, bringing a steady increase in the flow of people and goods in and out. The Heian capital was well on its way to becoming a mass city some eight hundred years before the walls of London and Paris came down.

THE DELIBERATE SECULARIZATION OF JAPANESE CITIES

The sixteenth and seventeenth centuries saw the deliberate creation of mass cities throughout Japan. Until then, Japanese cities large and small had maintained some connection to temples or shrines. In Kyoto, for example, the divinities of Kiyomizu Temple and Yasaka Shrine were venerated by the people as their "gods." In Kamakura, Tsurugaoka Hachimangū Shrine was placed at the city center; and the citizens of the "free city" of Sakai were fervent followers of the Buddhist Hokke and Zen sects.

But the warlords who became regional leaders amid the turmoil of the sixteenth century by, for instance, overthrowing their superiors had little religious inclination. Oda Nobunaga, the last in a line of such figures, did away with the power of the most influential religious sects of the time, and eliminated all religious influence from his new capital at Azuchi. Next he set out to cut the long-standing links between merchants and religious institutions, moving the merchants to the capital. He also introduced a policy of strict separation of the warrior and peasant classes, and as a start removed the retainers who lived in his native Owari from their estates to the capital, where he appointed them officials. He even went so far as to set fire to the homes of recalcitrant retainers who refused to follow his orders. With these steps he created Azuchi from the ground up as a mass dwelling group composed of merchants and the officials in charge of their regulation. A dwelling without gods had become the capital of the domain. This is how the birth of the first planned mass city came about.

Toyotomi Hideyoshi followed Nobunaga's lead in his capital at Fushimi Momoyama. Tokugawa Ieyasu then used the Azuchi/ Momoyama model to create mass cities across the nation. Under Ieyasu's policy of "one castle per realm," more than 260 castle towns were built and made the centers of their respective realms.

Walled castles were important fixtures in these towns, but amounted to little more than the leader's residence and symbol of the realm's management; they were not actual political strongholds embracing the populace. In fact, it was the districts located outside the castle walls, where merchants and artisans lived, that evolved into today's mass cities.

Among the Japanese cities which can be said to trace their origins back to these early Edo castle towns are Tokyo, Osaka, all the prefectural capitals, and most large and medium-sized cities surviving today. What's more, these towns' basic framework and structure have survived practically unchanged these last four centuries.

Even the external trappings of popular culture have adapted to the times rather than changing fundamentally. The former *teragoya*, or temple schools, were updated to become today's educational system. Palanquins were replaced by rickshaws and then taxis; the courier gave way to the postman. Some small saké-drinking spots (*izakaya*) evolved into bars, and the assignation-teahouse became the love hotel.

In comparison to mass cities in other areas of the world—often troubled by military threats and internal strife—Japan's castle towns enjoyed a high degree of stability. Moreover, the social system that made this possible has survived, albeit in various guises, to the present day. The key point of the system was the fact that the warriors, or samurai, doubled as government officials. As such, they invested their sense of pride and purpose in the management of their realms, or, more bluntly, the people of their realms. The samurai, with their high behavioral and ethical standards, may in the long run have helped form the basis for the so-called national character, known for its seriousness, studiousness, attention to cleanliness, and heavy sense of responsibility.

THE VITALITY OF JAPANESE MASS CITIES

It is no coincidence that the most common Japanese word for a city today is *toshi*, a compound consisting of the ancient word for "city" and the word for "market." In addition to being the seat of each realm's government, castle towns were successful business districts. With the ambitious merchants as a propelling force, and the conservative samurai officials applying the brakes, the towns were able to move forward into the future like a well-designed machine. Even as their vitality grew with leaps and bounds, they never lost their basic stability. And just as the powerful merchants of the past served as purveyors to the government, the links between the worlds of business and public administration remain extremely strong today.

I believe the most salient characteristic of Japan's "planned mass cities" is a sense of values that emphasizes vitality and efficiency, in the economic sphere as in all other things. We might say it is a society based on a "flow" rather than a "stock" mentality.

One example of this can be found in the willingness of Japanese architects to see their creations torn down every decade or so to make room for something new. Western architects are often shocked at this attitude, but for the Japanese the practice not only ensures up-to-date buildings suited to the times, but provides endless opportunities for up-and-coming young architects.

Non-Japanese visitors, and even Japanese returning from their first trip to the West, tend to criticize Japanese cities for their ugliness, poor housing, lack of greenery, unimpressive architecture, and high prices. If you were to look down at Tokyo from a high building, you would likely be dismayed by the haphazard jumble of wooden houses and concrete buildings of all shapes and sizes, the cluttered roofs adding to the chaos with a confusion of cooling towers, billboards, advertisements, electric wires, television antennas, little shrines, and other miscellaneous appendages. Seen from below the view is not much better.

On closer examination, however, Japanese cities do have their redeeming features. They are comparatively safe, especially in comparison to many Western cities where one cannot walk alone at night. They are clean. Even Osaka, sometimes called the "cuspidor of Japan," has been described as a clean and sanitary city by foreign visitors.

Japanese cities are also convenient. Transportation facilities are state-of-the-art; there are bullet trains between Tokyo and Osaka every fifteen minutes, and private railways are highly advanced. Variety shops, convenience stores, and public telephones are to be found everywhere in urban neighborhoods. I once had a terrible time trying to find a public telephone in London. Everywhere I looked, including the post office, there were either no public phones, or they were out of order.

Japanese cities are exciting and fun—certainly never boring. And finally, they are relatively free of rigid social stratification. There are no economic, professional, or intellectual "classes" so elite that their members would feel embarrassed to be seen in a pachinko parlor, or eating *takoyaki* dumplings bought from a vendor on the street.

What all these attributes finally boil down to is vitality.

In the past four hundred years since Nobunaga's Azuchi, Japan's castle-town-style mass cities have not only maintained their vibrant quality, but have come to function as the foundation and core of Japanese society as a whole. Although they have undergone many changes in the course of their encounters with European and American civilization, they have, as we have seen, continued to preserve the basic structure and value system that keep their vitality and stability in balance despite overwhelming population densities.

Finally, I would like to point out an area in which modern mass cities have made phenomenal progress unparalleled by anything in eras past—the information media. New media technology has brought the telegraph, telephone, radio, television, photocopier, facsimile, and personal computer into people's homes and offices, rendering today's mass communication practically omnipotent. Information obtained from the "gods" no longer accounts for even a hundredth of the total volume. At most, it consists of little more than the *omikuji*, the sacred lots people draw when they visit shrines at the New Year. For purposes of disseminating information, the mass media have become the new gods. The most powerful "oracles" known to society today are the trends generated by the mass cities.

GLOSSARY OF JAPANESE TERMS AND
PROMINENT HISTORICAL FIGURES

• *ashi-arai-ba*
pleasure quarter within precincts of
a shrine.

• *bakufu*
military dictatorship; the feudal government (=shogunate).

• *chawan*
rice bowl; dishes in general.

• *chaya*
traditional teahouse.

• *chōnai*
town block, neighborhood.

• *chōnai-kai*
town-block association.

• *daimyō*
lords; warlords.

• *demae*
home delivery service of simple one-
dish meals such as noodles in soup
or rice dishes.

• *donburi*
large porcelain bowl used for noodles in soup or flavored rice topped
with various ingredients.

• *donburi-mono*
simple meal consisting of flavored
rice topped with various ingredients.

• *ebisu*
drifting stranger-god.

• *en-taku*
"one-yen taxi," popular in late 1920s,
which charged a fixed fare within a
specific area.

• *furin*
"illicit" sexual relationship in which
one or both partners are married to
someone else; a temporary sexual
affair or fling.

• *furo*
Japanese hot-tub bath.

• *furoya*
public bathhouse.

• *Furuta Oribe*
(1544–1615) feudal lord, tea master,
originator of designs in tableware
and textiles.

• *gaijin*
present-day casual expression for a
foreigner.

• *gaikokujin*
foreigner, person from another country.

• *gei*
art.

• *geisha*
female performer of traditional
dance and musical arts, trained to
entertain individuals or small
groups.

• *Genji Monogatari*
Tale of Genji, famous Heian-period
novel.

• *go*
the national board game of Japan.

• *gyōsei shido*
administrative guidance; discre-
tionary authority of public officials.

• *hachi*
bowl for food other than soup or plain rice.

• *hadaka-kashi*
"no-frills" rental housing in Edo period: renters provided their own tatami floor-mats, stove, sliding panels, and other fittings.

• *hagaki*
an early form of paper currency.

• *hakama*
long Japanese-style skirt or divided skirt.

• *han*
feudal domain.

• *hansatsu*
paper currency issued by feudal domains.

• *haori*
coat worn with kimono.

• *harakiri*
suicide by disembowelment (=seppuku).

• *Hideyoshi*
see Toyotomi Hideyoshi.

• *Hishikawa Moronobu*
(died 1694) ukiyo-e painter, originator of ukiyo woodblock print.

• *hōbiki*
a form of gambling dating back to the Muromachi period (see tsuji-hōbiki).

• *iemoto*
individual or family that heads a "school" offering non-academic courses of lessons to the general public.

• *Ieyasu*
see Tokugawa Ieyasu.

• *Ihara Saikaku*
(1642–93) early Edo-period writer and poet, based in Osaka.

• *iro-naoshi*
change-of-costume by bride, or bride and groom, during wedding reception.

• *jinrikisha*
rickshaw, jinrickshaw.

• *Kabuki*
1. traditional dramatic form of premodern origin.
2. premodern aesthetic concept, used broadly to describe unconventional art forms, dress, etc.

• *kabuki-mono*
same as Kabuki.

• *kabu-nakama*
trade association, guild.

• *kago*
palanquin.

• *kaiseki-ryōri*
formal Japanese-style full course dinner.

• *kaisha*
company; corporation; firm.

• *Kansai*
region of Japan loosely centered around Osaka, Kyoto, and Kobe.

• *Kantō*
region of Japan loosely centered around Tokyo.

• *karaoke*
a recent, greatly popular recreational activity in which participants take turns singing well-known songs to pre-recorded instrumental accompaniment.

• *kawara-ban*
Edo-period tile block print newssheet consisting of picture and text.

• *ken*
linear measure (1.82 meters).

• *kibyōshi*
illustrated story book with yellow covers.

• *kimono*
Japanese-style clothing consisting of a long robe, sash, and accessories, dating back to Edo-period urban society.

• *kissaten*
coffee shop serving Western hot and cold beverages; may also serve desserts and light meals.

• *kō*
club; association; guild.

• *koken*
deed of sale.

• *koken-chi*
land privately owned by commoners in Edo period.

• *koken-ezu*
Edo-period charts listing details of privately owned land.

• *kosode*
wadded silk robe worn underneath wide-sleeved costume of nobles; precursor of kimono.

• *kudarimono*
high-quality products, including textiles, made in Kyoto and sent to Tokyo.

• *kumi*
group; financial group; association.

• *kuruwa-kotoba*
Edo-period "pleasure quarter language."

• *machi-buro*
neighborhood public bathhouses of medieval times.

• *machi-chi*
town land; land available for ownership by merchants and artisans, located outside the castle walls of Edo-period towns.

• *machigumi*
unit of urban community.

• *machi-kōba*
small factory in an urban neighborhood.

• *maiko*
apprentice geisha.

• *marebito*
ancient term meaning an "unusual visitor."

• *mochi*
glutinous rice cakes.

• *mon*
old monetary unit.

• *Moronobu*
see Hishikawa Moronobu.

• *mukotori-kon*
Heian-period marriage in which groom was adopted into bride's family.

• *mukōzuke*
bowls or plates for side dishes accompanying rice (excluding soup bowl).

• *nagaya*
tenement house; row house.

• *nakagai*
broker.

• *natsu-mero*
nostalgic melody.

• *Nobunaga*
see Oda Nobunaga.

• *noren*
sign curtain of eatery or public bathhouse.

• *nuke-mairi*
a form of Edo-period pilgrimage practiced by women, children, servants, apprentices, and so on who lacked the means or permission to make a regular pilgrimage.

• *o-ashi*
colloquial word for "money."

• *obi*
sash for kimono.

• *Oda Nobunaga*
(1534–82) warlord who began the process of unifying Japan under military dictatorship.

• *ofuro*
honorific form of "furo," Japanese hot-tub bath.

• *okage-mairi*
"freeloading pilgrimage," a term used to describe the situation where people would join nuke-mairi pilgrims to take advantage of alms and hospitality.

• *o-kane*
polite word for "money."

• *o-keiko-goto*
nonacademic courses of lessons in various disciplines for the general public.

• *okusan*
polite way to address or refer to a married woman (used only by samurai class in Edo period, but now used generally).

• *onna-gata*
male Kabuki actors specializing in female roles.

• *oyako-donburi*
flavored rice topped with egg and chicken mixture.

• *pachinko*
popular pinball-like game.

• *pakku ryokō*
package tour.

• *purehabu jūtaku*
prefabricated housing.

• *rāmen*
Chinese-style noodles in soup.

• *rin*
monetary unit (= 1/1000 yen) no longer in use.

• *Rikyū*
see Sen no Rikyū.

• *rintaku*
pedicab; trishaw.

• *ryō*
old monetary unit.

• *Saikaku*
see Ihara Saikaku.

• *saké*
Japanese rice wine.

• *samisen*
see shamisen.

• *samurai*
warrior; member of warrior class.

• *sara-chi*
new land ready to be built on.

• *satsu*
paper currency.

• *sen*
monetary unit (= 1/100 yen) no longer in use.

• *Sen no Rikyū*
(1521–91) founder of Senke school of tea ceremony.

• *sensei*
broad term of respect for a teacher, master, professor, instructor, doctor, person in authority, elected government official.

• *seppuku*
ritual suicide by disembowelment (=harakiri).

• *shamisen*
also samisen. three-stringed, long-necked, guitarlike Japanese traditional instrument, played with a plectrum.

• *shidashi*
home delivery service of full course meals, or one or more dishes for a full course meal.

• *shin-shinshūkyō*
neo-religion (sometimes "new-new religion"): a religious sect or cult formed after World War II.

• *shinshūkyō*
new religion, especially one that was started in the nineteenth or twentieth century prior to World War II.

• *Shinto*
Japanese animistic religion, closely associated with the imperial family.

• *shisatsu*
an early form of paper currency.

• *shitamachi*
commercial and entertainment district of Edo-period town or city.

• *shōgi*
Japanese chess.

• *shogun*
generalissimo, commander-in-chief (used since eighth century); hereditary military dictator (Kamakura through Edo periods).

• *shogunate*
office of the shogun; military dictatorship; the feudal government (=bakufu).

• *Shōtoku Taishi*
(574-622) Prince Shōtoku: imperial regent and de facto ruler of Japan, known for promotion of Buddhism and introduction of a constitution based on Confucian principles.

• *sodai gomi*
bulky garbage item.

• *sumo*
traditional Japanese wrestling, the national sport of Japan.

• *sushi*
vinegared rice with various ingredients.

• *sushi-oke*
flat lacquerware container for sushi.

• *takushi*
taxi.

• *taryōmono*
Edo-period term for person from another domain.

• *tashika na ie*
respectable household.

• *tatami*
straw-mat flooring.

• *Tokugawa Ieyasu*
(1542–1616) warlord who succeeded Toyotomi Hideyoshi, and founded the Tokugawa shogunate in 1603; the first Tokugawa shogun.

• *ton'ya*
wholesaler.

• *Toyotomi Hideyoshi*
(1536–98) warlord who succeeded Oda Nobunaga and completed the process of unifying Japan under military dictatorship.

• *tsuji-hōbiki*
a form of roadside gambling similar to a lottery, popular in Edo period.

• *tsutsusode*
tight-sleeved garment worn by the urban commoners whose work required freedom of arm movement.

• *ukiyo*
(lit. "floating world") Edo-period key word for prevalent tendency to seek momentary pleasure as an escape from the hardships of everyday life.

• *ukiyo-buro*
a type of Edo-period bathhouse with a higher percentage of hot water to steam than earlier types.

• *ukiyo-e*
Edo-period woodblock prints depicting contemporary life.

• *unagi*
eel.

- *unagi-donburi*
flavored rice topped with broiled eel.

- *yamate*
uptown districts for samurai residences in Edo-period towns and cities.

- *yen*
current Japanese monetary unit.

- *yome-iri-kon*
a marriage in which bride enters groom's family.

- *yomi-uri*
street vendors selling kawara-ban.

- *yūgei*
recreational arts.

- *yukata*
long, unlined cotton robe used for lounging and festival wear.

- *yuna*
young woman employed by yuna-buro (see below).

- *yuna-buro*
a type of Edo-period bathhouse employing young women to bathe and entertain customers.

- *zainichi gaikokujin*
foreign resident of Japan.

- *zaru-soba*
cold buckwheat noodle dish.

- *zei, zeikin*
tax.

LIST OF CONTRIBUTORS

Kayoko Aikawa	Professor of history of costume, Department of Culture and Humanities, Nara Women's University.
Shin'ya Hashizume	Lecturer of architectural history and Urban Planning, Kyoto Seika University.
Tsutomu Hayama	Lecturer, Department of Architecture, Kyoto Seika University.
Masahiro Hikita	Executive Director, Communication Design Institute, Kyoto.
Takahiro Hisa	Assistant professor of urban planning and design, Osaka University.
Shōichi Inoue	Associat professor, history of architecture and theory of design, International Research Center for Japanese Studies, Kyoto.
Naomichi Ishige	Professor of ethnology, National Museum of Ethnology, Osaka.
Atsushi Katagi	Associate professor, Department of Architecture, Nagoya University.
Akinori Kato	Associate professor of environmental design, Department of Environmental Engineering, Osaka University.
Kōji Miyake	Assistant professor of history of science and technology, Osaka Kyōiku University.
Katsuhisa Moriya	Professor of Japanese history, Mukogawa Women's University, Hyōgo Prefecture.
Takeshi Moriya	Former professor of ethnology, National Museum of Ethnology, Osaka. Died in 1991.
Kunihiro Narumi	Professor of environmental planning, Department of Environmental Engineering, Faculty of Engineering, Osaka University.
Günter Nitschke	Director of Institute for East Asian Architecture and Urbanism, Kyoto.

Yōtarō Sakudō	Professor of Japanese economic history, Osaka International University.
Osamu Tabata	Professor of urban planning and design, Osaka University of Arts.
Masatoshi Takada	Professor of tourism study, Mukogawa Women's University, Hyōgo Prefecture.
Yasuo Takahashi	Associate professor of architecture, Kyoto University.
Atsuko Tanaka	Lecturer on architecture, Department of Art, Kyoto Seika University.
Atsushi Ueda	Professor of architecture, Kyoto Seika University.
Toshio Yokoyama	Associate professor of modern history, Institute for Research in Humanities, Kyoto University.
Toshinao Yoneyama	Professor, Department of Cultural Anthropology, Faculty of Integrated Human Studies, Kyoto University.
Shōji Yoshino	Professor of housing and design, Bukkyo University, Kyoto.
Takao Yoshii	Associate professor of Japanese history, Hanazono University, Kyoto.

Michitarō Tada and Yoshisuke Nakaoka also participated in this project.